ACCESS TO SCHOOL

An innovative two-generation school readiness approach to empowering immigrant parents

For more information, visit

BibToBackpack.org

ISBN: 978-1-942011-26-2

Version 1.0

Cover art and design by Rick Nease

www.RickNeaseArt.com

Published by ACCESS

Publishing services provided by Front Edge Publishing, LLC

For information about customized editions, bulk purchases or
permissions, contact Front Edge Publishing, LLC at
info@FrontEdgePublishing.com

assisting. improving. empowering.

United Way
for Southeastern Michigan

Contents

"A wise teacher leads you to the threshold of your own mind. ...

"Your children are the sons and daughters of Life's longing for itself ...

"For their souls dwell in the house of tomorrow."

Kahlil Gibran, *the great Lebanese-American poet (1883-1931) who was brought to this country by his mother at age 12. Although she was poor and worked hard to support her family, young Kahlil's life was transformed by immediately starting English as a Second Language classes at the family's neighborhood public school.*

This book is dedicated to all of the parents working to create a better life for their children through the educational opportunities that they themselves did not have.

View video at: http://bit.ly/1UckILh

Welcome!

This is the story of how professionals from our nonprofit, ACCESS, developed an innovative school-readiness program for an especially challenging community in Southeast Michigan, where many families are recent immigrants from non-English-speaking parts of the world.

We are sharing our story, including some of the unexpected challenges we faced along the way, in the hope that readers will learn from our accomplishments. We invite you, the reader, to use this as a helpful guide in developing your own programs in communities nationwide. As is the case for most nonprofits, the need is there and the work is happening long before the funding arrives. ACCESS had been running most of the program components for many years, but I began seeking out an opportunity to build upon and strengthen this work to better meet the needs of our focus community. In this case, the grant proposal went to the Social Innovation Fund (SIF) of the Corporation for National and Community Service, managed by United Way for Southeastern Michigan. As we launched our SIF program, called ACCESS to School, we developed four distinct components: English as a Second Language, Parenting Education, Case Management and - the most innovative part of the program - Parent and Child Interactive Learning.

While the specific program described in this book is new, it is part of a much longer mission at ACCESS, which was founded in 1971 and was known for years as Arab Community Center for Economic and Social Services. For nearly half a century, ACCESS has been in the "business of engaging and empowering communities." Today, our organization is known simply as ACCESS, and we work with families from all racial, ethnic and religious backgrounds. Throughout our history, we have understood that education is the cornerstone of any thriving community. We are experienced in this field and, before ACCESS to School, we sponsored other programs to help children succeed in school - and beyond.

Many scholarly studies link early childhood education to long-term improvements in academic success, higher educational attainment and even reduced likelihood of delinquency, as children grow into adulthood. That's why we have been putting a lot of effort into developing and improving school-readiness programs. We take this work very seriously and follow best practices, which includes having our work analyzed by an independent evaluation team. We know that this work has long-lasting effects in the lives of children and their families - and leads to long-term change in communities.

Working through the Social Innovation Fund, our ACCESS to School Program was a challenging journey over a number of years that led to major changes in the way we approach school readiness with immigrant parents and their children. Through community-needs assessments, the piloting of different curricula and trials and errors in instructional delivery, we learned the limitations of most existing programs and curricula for school readiness. These existing programs are appropriately designed for the English-speaking population, but are too fast-paced and the vocabulary too difficult for a population with limited English language skills. In addition, although there are many early learning curricula available, few of them are two-generation models, and virtually no two-generation models that we are able to find are specific to a population of recent immigrants.

We believe that two-generation learning models are crucial, since studies have shown that one of the main determinants for a child's academic success is the reading level of the child's mother. Our team followed an extensive process in developing ACCESS to School in order to meet the challenges of the local population and to maintain our commitment to include both parents and children in the learning process.

Our empowerment-based, hybrid program incorporates four components:

- Adult English as a Second Language (ESL) programming - where participants in ESL classes form the larger population from which we can invite eligible parents with children into the other three components of ACCESS to School.
- Case Management - assistance for those families who continue into the next two components of the program.
- Tailored Parenting Education.
- Parent and Child Interactive Learning (PCIL) - the center of our greatest overall innovation and the phase of the program you will learn about most extensively in this book.

There are many innovative pieces to each of these components, but educators, funders and external evaluators who observed our program were particularly impressed with our PCIL component, and encouraged us to share that story with the world through this book.

The innovation and success of PCIL lies in its three key elements:

- Early Learning Content - a curriculum that incorporates the alphabet, shapes, colors, comparisons and more.
- Parent-Child Interaction - an initiative that helps parents to practice techniques for teaching their children.
- Awareness - working with the parents to become aware of their child's development and learning, and the importance of becoming their child's first teacher.

These elements have led to significant growth in our children's kindergarten readiness. In this book, we invite you to walk with us through our process of innovation. We will show you lesson plans from the Parent and Child Interactive Learning portion of our program. We will take you through a typical day in our work with parents and children. And, you will meet some of the families whose lives have changed through ACCESS to School.

If the U.S. Census projection is accurate, by 2040, 50 percent of America's youth will be the children of immigrant parents. It is our hope that this book will inspire you to develop programs in your own region that will guide our future leaders, giving them a head start in life through quality early education.

Enjoy!

- Anisa Sahoubah, Director of the Youth and Education Department at ACCESS

Spring 2016

http://www.accesscommunity.org

Nahed Alkashbari helps Layla Assofe with an assignment.

Our Story

From Anisa Sahoubah, director of the Youth and Educa-tion Department at ACCESS:

When I heard about the Corporation for National and Community Service's Social Innovation Fund, I knew that our organization had an opportunity to help families in one of the most challenging communities we serve. That's an area in Detroit where many Hispanic-American and Yemeni-American families are recent immigrants with limited English language skills, low incomes and low levels of education overall.

In writing the original proposal for our grant, I drew on the demographic expertise that ACCESS has utilized over the years in developing over 100 programs and services housed in 10 facilities throughout metropolitan Detroit. As I created this new proposal and began assembling a team to organize this pro-gram–starting with Amanda Morgan–I understood that this new program had to overcome major barriers. We were focusing on an area of recent immigrants, many of whom are culturally conservative and socially isolated. We faced a challenge in sim-ply convincing children and their parents that their local schools are welcoming places where they can learn and build commu-nity relationships. Working with families to help children enter kindergarten with the cognitive, social, emotional and language skills needed to succeed has always been part of ACCESS' main goals. Over many years, ACCESS has operated a wide range of programs aimed at teaching language skills and assisting fam-ilies with the school readiness of their children. But, with the Social Innovation Fund, we had a chance to develop a new kind of approach to having parents learn alongside their children, in a two-generation component within our new ACCESS to School

Program: Parent and Child Interactive Learning (PCIL). This approach is aimed at empowering the parents themselves to become their children's first teachers, first in our classrooms and then in the home. As we made our plans, we drew on the growing body of research that shows the effectiveness of this kind of multi-generational learning that empowers parents to take on a crucial early role in their children's education.

While that idea sounds ideal, many parents in our focus community simply were not equipped to serve as their children's first teachers. They felt they had little time in their demanding daily schedules to help their children with lessons. In fact, many of them had not given much thought to themselves in this new role, for which we hoped to provide training. Many parents in this community assumed that by coming to this country, struggling through long, hard days to make a living for their families and then eventually sending their children to local schools, they were fulfilling their mission as parents to educate the next generation. As we developed our program, we looked at extensive demographic research showing high levels of poverty and illiteracy among the adults in this community, including overall low levels of educational achievement among the adults. These findings guided the development of our program to begin with a population of adults we would welcome into English as a Second Language classes. The ACCESS to School Program would further offer parents an opportunity for parenting education, Case Management and–for parents with appropriately aged children – our PCIL component. Our comprehensive program also was aligned with United Way for Southeastern Michigan's goal of preparing children to enter kindergarten with the cognitive, emotional, social and language skills needed to succeed. Together, as our grant proposal was accepted, ACCESS and United Way became a part of the nationwide network of programs fostered by the Social Innovation Fund.

As you read about the development of our efforts in Detroit, it's important to keep in mind that families vary widely in their educational backgrounds. While many immigrants come to the US with advanced degrees, others come with limited to no formal schooling. Although many of the immigrant families in our focus community have low educational levels, it was clear to me that they value education and are desperately looking for ways to support their children and to provide them with the educational opportunities that they themselves did not have access to.

Horace Mann, a great educational reformer, once said "education is the great equalizer." I am a firm believer in this statement, and in the belief that education is what lifts people out of poverty, increases their opportunities, and allows them to reach their full potential. Through my 18 years of experience working with several immigrant communities, I came to realize that the majority of these immigrants held these same beliefs – it was circumstances that prevented them from attaining their educational goals (war, geography, early marriage, taking care of elders, etc.) – not doubt in the importance of education.

Our learners are often surprised when I tell them that I am also an immigrant, and are amused when I tell them the story of how – even as a 5-year-old coming from Yemen – I was very self-conscious of my inability to speak English, and wondered out loud to my parents as soon as we landed in the US, how I was going to learn this "strange" language that everyone seemed to be speaking at Detroit Metro Airport. They laugh at this story, but also make a valid point when they tell me to imagine how magnified their struggles are – to come in as adults with many other responsibilities and insecurities, and are expected to navigate life in their new country in a very short amount of time.

It is this knowledge of the specific challenges that adult immigrants with limited English skills face that led me to expand the work that ACCESS was doing with school-aged children to include programs and services that will empower their parents to succeed as well. The development and expansion was gradual, but developed into what we now call "Adult and Family Learning." This includes six levels of English as a Second Language classes, parenting, health and nutrition, U.S. Citizenship test preparation, computer training, and several other programs designed to equip parents with the skills they need to help their children, and to reach their own personal and professional goals.

As you read our story, if you are considering working with recent immigrant families, it's important to avoid making universal assumptions about any ethnic group. As we did at ACCESS, anyone approaching this kind of work needs to begin with a careful demographic analysis of each local population so that community needs can be pinpointed, and programming, approach, and delivery can be modified to meet those needs. This will ultimately lead to a bigger impact on the individuals served, over a shorter timeframe.

Who are Arab Americans?

Arab Americans are U.S. citizens or permanent residents who trace their ancestry to, or who immigrated from, Arabic-speaking places in the Middle East. Not all people in this region are Arabs. Most Arab Americans were born in the United States. A 2013 report by the U.S. Census Bureau stated that the number of people saying they had Arab ancestry grew 76 percent, from 850,000 in 1990 to an estimated 1.5 million in 2006-2010. However, the Arab American Institute, based on its own research, estimates that this population is closer to five million. Arab Americans live in all 50 states. According to the U.S. Census Bureau, about one-third are in California, Michigan and New York. Another one-third are in seven states: Illinois, Maryland, Massachusetts, New Jersey, Ohio, Texas and Virginia.

Source: *100 Questions & Answers About Arab Americans.* Michigan State University School of Journalism, 2014.

From Nahed Alkashbari, case manager, teacher of the Parent and Child Interactive Learning (PCIL) and parenting education classes, and co-creator of the PCIL curriculum:

My inspiration for my work at ACCESS stems from my upbringing overseas, love for cultures and passion to empower women. Aden, where I was born and raised, is a fountain of inspiration for my work. It is a former British colony located in south Yemen, bordering the Red Sea and the Gulf of Aden. Its location and rich international history have made it an important international harbor in south Yemen. Growing up in a city where education is the key to success, I have a drive to inspire my love of knowledge in women whose upbringings did not promote education. I believe that cultivating this love of knowledge in the Yemeni-American women around me will empower their sense of independence in navigating the English-speaking world, in raising a child, in being strong women. The Yemeni-American families we serve with ACCESS to School come from different parts of Yemen – smaller villages where education, especially for women, is neither accessible nor encouraged.

Like many families from Aden, my father and several relatives worked in management at the harbor. My family understood the value of training and education, so all of us – including the women – were expected to graduate college. This attitude toward education was typical in the city of Aden, even in the 70s, when I was raised. People in Aden knew that everyone had to go to school: education was for boys and girls alike. There was no difference. Our parents would tell us that school is the doorway for everywhere you hope to go in your life. We had lots of books in our home. I still remember a ritual that I enjoyed until I went to college: every Thursday afternoon, my father, brothers and sisters would sit together as we waited for my father to bring out newspapers and magazines. We sat and read together all afternoon and into the late evening. We read about everything from sports to world politics. And, most importantly, we would discuss what we had read. To emphasize: My family, our curiosity, wasn't exceptional – we were a typical family in Aden at that time. My sisters and brothers all graduated college and even went on for advanced degrees.

I attended Sana'a University, where I studied education, majoring in English. I was trained to teach English as a Second Language, but I did not immediately work as a teacher. I first worked for several international agencies, including UNICEF in Yemen. It was always my dream to come to America. It's a better place for women – truly a land of opportunity, where women can pursue higher education and professional opportunities. I first came to America in 1999. When I moved to Dearborn, Michigan, to further my education, I quickly became involved in the Yemeni community. I realized the disparity of resources available for parents and their children and a gap between parents and their children in their attitude toward learning and social norms.

Many of the families who make this long journey to America from Yemen or Mexico come to communities where they have friends or family who can help them adjust. These friends and families formed Yemeni-American and Hispanic-American communities around Priest Elementary School, where I currently teach the parenting classes and PCIL components. I was working for another agency in 2012, when Anisa called me and said, "I have the perfect job for you. It's going to be very rewarding, and you'll be working with women you can understand and relate to because they, too, are from Yemen." I applied for the position, knowing it would fulfill my passion to empower women through education. Soon, I began working with Amanda Morgan, the supervisor for the Adult and Family Learning department at ACCESS, to structure this program.

While we were excited and prepared for the road ahead, we were constantly surprised by challenges we faced. The majority of the women participating in PCIL are from Yemen, but their family experiences were different from my own or from Anisa's. Many of them had lived in villages in the countryside and worked on farms. In these families, education for girls was not a priority. Education, for them, was mainly for boys. Beliefs in these villages were not the only limitation to girls' access to education. Schools are located far away from their homes. Only boys were entrusted to walk these distances for school. If girls were permitted to travel these distances, the majority were only allowed to complete third or fourth grade. Many women in PCIL program echo this: "Oh, my family thought school was too far away for girls to go."

In these communities, most girls are expected to work at home and spend their time with their mothers learning how to run a household. For a lot of these women, working at home also meant working in the fields, cultivating corn, bulgur wheat and vegetables. They also took care of the family's livestock and often carried water from wells in barrels each day. The farming and household work consumed their lives. Even when these women move away from the village to the cities in the United States, they are charged with the care of many family members. Their new multi-generational homes in the United States are filled with parents, grandparents, young adults and children. Living with so many people under one roof, the women are always busy with housework.

Inundated with busy households, these women have little opportunity to develop their academic skills and find it difficult to justify leaving their demanding homes for school. The pull of household work and childrearing is so strong that some women have lived in the U.S. for over 10 years and speak very little English. Aside from household chores, some women are faced with the challenge of attending school for the first time in their lives when they participate in our programs. A lack of schooling presents more challenges – identifying learning strengths, weaknesses, and even disabilities. Some women in our program are very recent arrivals. They begin working with us within months of arriving from Yemen. While they face similar challenges (language, household obligations, cultural approach to education) as women who have been here for a long time, new arrivals also face a difficult adjustment period to America and to Metro Detroit.

Our program helps women of all backgrounds navigate a new or different culture. Specifically, we focus on bridging the gap between the parents and their children in education. Faced with assimilation and socioeconomic challenges, Yemeni-American parents often believe that finding their children a good school is enough. We often hear: "We came to America so we could send our children to a good school to get an education. We're not teachers. We send them to school for that." These parents do not realize that education begins at an early age – years before school begins. The mothers, especially, unfamiliar with the educational system, do not understand their impact on their children's education. The gap in interaction is evident even in these mothers' involvement in outdoor activities, such as taking their children to the park. They tend to keep their children, so full of energy, inside the house. This further exhausts the women and creates a life that is largely limited to running the household.

The challenges that the women face on a daily basis – household chores, limited access to resources, and childrearing – have made location a necessary consideration in structuring this program. Thus, our program is located near their homes and provides transportation. Furthermore, we provide childcare so the mothers have more flexibility.

I have spoken about some of the challenges that Amanda Morgan and I had to overcome. We continue to address the obstacles and joys we encounter, step by step as we continue to develop this program, meeting each of the needs we identify. We know that in order to make this a safe learning community, we must do our best to care for the concerns of these women and their children.

The well-roundedness of our program has made it accessible and applicable to the Hispanic women of the Priest community as well. At first, I was unsure of the success of a program that included women from such different places and backgrounds. I was aware of their differences, but hadn't considered the similar challenges they faced. I also discovered that they were learning from each other. I remember the first time I saw a Yemeni and a Mexican woman sitting down side by side. When class ended, I saw them teach each other greetings and phrases like "Thank you" and "Good-Bye" in their native languages. This was not part of our lesson plan, but these women, on their own, were trying to communicate with each other and exploring their thirst for knowledge. Every day, I am further empowered and inspired by these strong, motivated women who overcome daily challenges just to get to school. They do it for themselves, for their children, for their community. I am so happy to be a part of their journey and the community at Priest.

Who are Hispanic Americans?

Hispanic, by definition, means "of Spain or Spanish-speaking countries." *Latino* means "from or related to Latin America." Some Spanish-speaking countries, such as Spain, are not in Latin America. Some Latin American countries, such as Brazil, are not Spanish-speaking. The U.S. Census Bureau began using the term "Hispanic" in some forms in 1970. The term "Latino" was added in 1997, and now both terms are used. The Pew Research Center's Hispanic Trends Project found that roughly half of the Hispanic and Latino people in the U.S. have no strong preference for either term – except in one state: Texas, where 46 percent said, in 2013, that they preferred to be called "Hispanic," while only 8 percent preferred "Latino." Though these Americans often are portrayed as immigrants, many Hispanics were actually living in this region long before it became the United States. In 2014, Hispanics made up almost one-fifth of the total U.S. population (17 percent), up from 13 percent in 2000.

Source: *100 Questions & Answers About Hispanics and Latinos*. Michigan State University School of Journalism, 2014.

From Amanda Morgan, supervisor for Adult and Family Learning programs at ACCESS and who developed and adapted the ACCESS to School Program in its current form (along with Nahed Alkashbari):

Our story really is a story of creative adaptation, learning from the families in this community and continually removing barriers we discovered along the way.

Even before Nahed was hired, Anisa showed me the grant proposal for the Social Innovation Fund – and we knew from the start that the focus of our innovation was going to be this approach to two-generation learning, empowering parents to become their children's first teachers. We would teach and coach the parents along with the children – showing the parents how they could become early teachers both in our classroom, where we could assist them, and then in the home after that. This idea was showing up in academic literature about approaches to school readiness and increasing early literacy for children.

But we were not seeing this idea in the form of an actual program that was appropriate for immigrant families. So, we had this important idea for a strategy and we had the grant, but there was a huge amount of work needed to actually turn this into a program with all of the components that we eventually developed.

I was brought in to lead this program because of my background in program planning and evaluation. I got my Masters of Social Work at the University of Michigan, where I specialized in program evaluation and community organizing. While I was completing my master's degree, I did my internship at ACCESS with their National Network for Arab American Communities (NNAAC). After I finished my MSW, I was hired by ACCESS, first to manage a home-visiting family prevention program in the community, and later brought in to manage ACCESS to School.

I had a lot to learn about the Arab American community when I originally began interning at ACCESS. This is a diverse community and there was a lot to learn about the international and historical context – as well as important issues for the Arab-American community in this country. But after years working at ACCESS, working directly with immigrant communities and advocating at a national level around issues and policies important to immigrant communities, I felt like I understood a lot about the challenges that we would face in this new program. Don't get me wrong, I don't believe that you can ever reach a "level of cultural competence" – you should always be focused on having humility and being willing to learn. But at the time, I felt as though I brought in a lot of good experience, and didn't fully anticipate the challenges we would have when building a program from the ground up, ensuring it met rigorous research and evaluation standards, while still meeting the needs of our focus community.

The focus community for our ACCESS to School Program, around Priest Elementary School in Southwest Detroit, is not far from ACCESS headquarters. I knew that this was primarily a Yemeni-American community. So, when Anisa asked me to take on the development of this new program, we had two major goals in mind: 1) create a program that addresses the specific needs of the community we would be serving, and 2) make sure that, with small modifications, it can be scaled and replicated with other immigrant communities across the country. Like I described earlier, I thought I had a pretty good handle on what the needs and barriers of an immigrant community would be, but I was quickly reminded that the needs of the community around Priest Elementary were specific and in some ways different from the larger Arab community. Anyone who tries to organize a program like this needs to think about the unique challenges you'll face when you bring a program like this to a very specific group of people.

As Anisa and I were discussing the community, I remember her saying, "My family came from a village in Yemen with limited educational opportunities, but I had the good fortune of coming to the U.S. at a young age and had very supportive parents." She continued on talking about the diversity in experiences of Yemeni people, that many have very high educational attainment, and others are not as fortunate. "Most of the women that we will be serving are typically arriving as adults, and back in Yemen they lived in rural villages, where they lacked opportunities to access formal education," she said. But it really wasn't until Nahed and I dove deep into the details of our program and the details of this community that we were able to start answering questions like: Why should the program be designed like this? What are the strengths of these women? What are the needs of these women – and why do they have these needs? The issue wasn't that these women were from Yemen. In fact, many women in the program are Hispanic American. The real issue was that these women, along with millions of women and girls around the world, do not have access to educational opportunities that they can then pass on to their children.

It's particularly frustrating when political leaders, and even officials in education and nonprofits, say they can't understand why these mothers aren't teaching their children at home and getting them ready for school. Because they *are* teaching their children! They are teaching them to speak a second language; they are teaching them about history, culture and community. They teach their children about being humble, kind, and charitable to others. But in this country there is a different expectation than in their home country: children must have a specific set of skills *before* beginning school vs. children are sent to school to learn these skills. Many of the women in our program are not aware of this expectation, do not feel that they have the skills and abilities to teach their children what they need to know, and/or many of them struggle themselves with these concepts in English. Being aware of these constructs helped us develop our program. There were challenges to designing our evaluation, as well as many barriers to them coming to class. It took all of us applying our knowledge and experience, learning more about the challenges and barriers that the community faced, and building off of the strengths of these women to create the successful program we have today.

1. English as a Second Language (ESL)

ACCESS to School's 4 components start with a pool of adults enrolled in ESL

2. Parenting Education

For parents with children ages 0-5

4. Case Management

3. PCIL: Parent and Child Interactive Learning

For parents with children ages 3-5

Early Learning Content

Colors, shapes, alphabet, numbers, counting, sizes, comparisons, rhyming, reading

PCIL is a safe learning community

Parent-Child Interaction

- Parent learns teaching techniques
- Parent teaches with supervision, building skills and confidence
- Child increases social skills, attention span, motor skills and reduces separation anxiety
- Promotes ongoing learning at home

Awareness of ...

- parents as first teachers at home
- parents' teaching abilities
- how children learn from birth
- children's stages of development
- school readiness as an ongoing goal

The Four Components of Our Program

From Amanda Morgan:

Many communities within Detroit face high poverty rates, high unemployment and high rates of adult illiteracy. Far too many children arrive at school scoring low in all areas of school readiness, including language development, approaches to learning, social and emotional development, cognition and general knowledge, and physical well-being and motor development. The research data on this challenge is extensive and very compelling. One of the greatest determinants for a child's academic success is the reading level of the child's mother – so our strategy is based on the goal of developing a family approach to a child's school readiness.

Detroit is a big city (143 square miles) with lots of diverse neighborhoods – and our ACCESS to School Program focuses on a very distinctive area called Southwest Detroit. This is a region within the city where immigrants from around the world have flocked for jobs and a better life for more than a century. It's not far from Henry Ford's Rouge complex, once the largest integrated factory in the world. Waves of Irish, Hungarian and other European immigrants filled this neighborhood and formed their own ethnic circles within Southwest Detroit. The Yemeni and Hispanic immigrants who migrated to this area are following a well-worn pathway that has produced leading figures in all fields of American life. In some ways, today's immigrants face decades-old challenges that millions of Americans recognize from the stories of their own ancestors. But today's immigrants also face some fresh barriers, including a widespread distrust of immigrants that has spread across America over the last decade or so.

The ACCESS to School Program is an empowerment-based approach to school readiness, which incorporates four components that address the needs of the population we serve:

1. Adult English as a Second Language programming
2. Culturally adapted Parenting Education

3. Parent and Child Interactive Learning

4. Comprehensive Case Management for the family

This forms a safe learning community. That means these components address the educational needs of the parents and children; the basic needs of the family (including working with them to set goals around sustainability); and the parents' need for empowerment and awareness in becoming their children's first teacher. In order to address the unique and complex challenges and barriers of the population, the program has to be comprehensive, culturally adapted and meet the specific needs and barriers present.

English as a Second Language (ESL)

Our ESL setting is a closed-enrollment, teacher-led classroom with approximately 25 learners in any class. Within the classroom, the teachers regularly use breakout groups and have the learners work as pairs. Learners are placed into one of our class levels – based on their skill level determined at intake – ranging from learners who are illiterate in their native language and do not know any English to learners who are a few semesters away from being ready to transition into a General Educational Development (GED) preparation class to reach high school equivalency. The overall goal of ACCESS's ESL classes are to help adult learners acquire the English skills they need to better function within their families, community and broader society.

Many of our adult learners come to our ESL classes with goals such as getting their U.S. citizenship, being able to talk to their doctor, getting their driver's license, wanting to help their child with homework or talk to their teacher and getting a job. A few have the goal of going on to receive GED certification and going to college. Some of the learners have been in America for five to 10 years and others have just arrived from their native countries. Although their goals, needs and challenges vary, our ESL classes are communicative, focus on navigating American culture and systems, use real materials and are flexible and responsive to the learners.

Three times per year, we open registration for the upcoming semester. Prospective learners go through an intake process that assesses their abilities in reading, writing, listening and speaking English, using the Comprehensive Adult Student Assessment System (CASAS) to place them in the correct class level.

During this intake process, learners are also screened for the ACCESS to School Program. If learners qualify for the ACCESS to School Program by having at least one child age 0-5, they speak with an ACCESS to School caseworker to discuss the benefits of the program. If learners wish to participate in the ACCESS to School Program, they are enrolled in the appropriate ESL class and also in the additional ACCESS to School components (Case Management, Parenting Education and PCIL). If parents cannot or do not choose to participate in the larger program, we thank them and place them in an appropriate ESL class where they continue only as an ESL student.

There are four levels of ESL offered every semester: Beginning Literacy; Level 1 (also known as High Beginning); Level 2 (Intermediate); and Level 3 (Advanced). Beginning Literacy focuses on memorizing basic nouns and verbs that surround our learners, survival English phrases, understanding basic sentence structure and utilizing foundational phonics skills. Once these skills have been mastered, learners may move to Level 1, where they are introduced to basic greetings and phrases, answering common questions and reading and writing common words that relate to a variety of situations encountered in their daily life. Level 2 focuses more on grammar, usage, sentence structure and more complex conversation skills, to build upon what was taught in the previous two levels. Level 3 is for learners who wish to further refine their reading, writing and speaking skills. Often, these learners have higher aspirations of obtaining employment or going on to higher education. In this class, learners study paragraph structure, contextual reading skills and conversational skills focusing on new vocabulary and pronunciation. We also offer two small group sessions each semester, as needed: Literacy Prep and Higher Ed. Prep. Literacy Prep comprises a small group (usually 4-10 learners) run by a volunteer instructor who prepares learners for Beginning Literacy. This class typically has older learners, learners who likely have learning disabilities and learners who never learned to read and write in their native language – all of whom need a slower pace and more one-on-one instruction. Higher Ed. Prep also comprises a small group (8-15) learners run by a volunteer instructor who teaches learners at the point when they are almost ready to move on to higher education and want more advanced material and more one-on-one time with an instructor.

ESL is a core component of the ACCESS to School Program for many reasons. Parents are expected to cultivate English language development in their children as a part of school readiness, and it's unreasonable to think that they can be expected to do this without having those basic skills themselves. ESL also gives parents the language skills needed to access necessary resources in getting their child ready for school, and to continue to remain engaged in their child's education. But underlying all of these things – giving parents the ability to speak for themselves, be successful, achieve their goals, interact with the world around them and advocate for themselves – sets the stage for these women to reach beyond their own homes and build a better community for all families.

✿❀❁

Case Management

As an agency, ACCESS believes that in order to create sustainable change, we must address the needs of the whole person within the context of their family and their community. At ACCESS, all programs function within a wrap-around services model: If a client has a crucial need that is not being met, that may cripple the effectiveness of our programs, so we try to ensure that clients can address these core needs. Because ACCESS offers so many programs and services, the need can often be met within ACCESS; at other times, ACCESS relies on its many partners in the community for other resources and referrals.

After a family agrees to participate in the ACCESS to School Program, a caseworker sets up an initial meeting with the parents, to fully explain both the program and what is expected of parents and children. The caseworker also assesses the specific strengths, needs and barriers within that family. If there are any basic needs that are not being met, such as food, housing, utilities, etc., the caseworker begins working to assist the family immediately. Otherwise, the caseworker talks to the parent about what Case Management involves and how it can be helpful, and tells them to start thinking about goals they want to set for themselves and their family during their time in the program.

At the next meeting, the caseworker checks in with the parents to see how the program has been going and whether or not they have any concerns or new challenges. Parents also are asked if they are in need of any resources or referrals at that time. After checking in, the caseworker sets goals with the parents. Parents may list as many goals as they would like, but they are required to identify at least one within the program. The goals are entirely self-directed by the parents and can be related to: basic needs (e.g., getting reliable transportation); parenting (e.g., using better discipline techniques); school readiness (e.g., reading more to my child); and their personal education (e.g., improving my English). The only requirements for the goals are that they be SMART (Specific, Measureable, Attainable, Relevant, Timebound) and that each goal can be broken down into specific action steps. The caseworker then guides parents through this process.

Throughout the program, the caseworker tracks each family and follows up, making at least one contact with them each month. The caseworker keeps track of their attendance in their classes and calls them if they are absent for an extended period of time, offering to help them remove barriers that are preventing them from coming to classes. Resources and referrals are given as needed throughout the program. The caseworker follows up with each parent about the progress they have made on their action steps and goals, gives them encouragement and offers help completing steps if needed.

Parenting Education

The ACCESS to School Parenting Education component is a hybrid starting with mainstream parenting education curricula and then blending in topics, examples, structure and a facilitation style that we know fits with our specific immigrant population. Although the core topics in widely used parenting education programs are relevant, the way they are presented and the examples given are often confusing or irrelevant to an immigrant population in general – and to our specific community in particular. Additionally, there are many topics missing in mainstream programs that are important to this population.

The mainstream parenting education curriculum we chose as our base is separated into seven topics:

1. Understanding Young Children
2. Understanding Young Children's Behavior
3. Building Self-Esteem in the Early Years
4. Listening and Talking to Young Children
5. Helping Young Children to Cooperate
6. Discipline for Young Children
7. Young Children's Social and Emotional Development

Immigrant parents have very specific needs in addition to the basic topics, such as: learning about parenting expectations in America as compared to their native countries; navigating language barriers within and outside of their families; dealing with variances in first- and second-generation immigrant issues with their children; and exploring the often new idea of co-parenting.

The basic curriculum we chose was structured as seven, two-hour sessions. Given our need to adapt to our community, the ACCESS to School Parenting Education component now comprises 24, one-hour sessions. This provides more time for explanations, translation/interpretation and breaking down complex words and concepts into forms that parents with little to no formal education can truly engage with. This format also gives parents the information in smaller doses during shorter class times, allowing them to go home in between classes and apply what they learned and then come back and discuss challenges and successes. This allows for more practice, discussion, reflection and peer support.

The most important characteristic of this class is creating a safe and comfortable environment. The class covers topics that are considered private family matters that many people in the community do not feel comfortable sharing with outsiders, so it is essential to have the teacher be a trusted member of the community who is skilled in facilitating sensitive topics, speaks the native language of the parents and is genuinely committed to creating a positive and supportive environment in the classroom. Although ESL and PCIL are taught in English because of the nature of the learning objectives, Parenting Education should be taught in the language the learners are most comfortable with, which will most likely be their native language. We have also found within this component that, if more than one native language is spoken in the class, it is ideal to have a volunteer, tutor or co-teacher who speaks the other language become a part of the class. In addition, we have all materials translated into both languages so everyone feels welcome and is able to fully engage in the class.

Parent and Child Interactive Learning (PCIL)

We made many adaptations in creating our overall ACCESS to School Program, but the PCIL component was created to address the specific needs of our focus community and is the core of our greatest innovation. As we did our planning, we explored the work of a number of scholars – especially psychologist Barbara Hanna Wasik, at the University of North Carolina at Chapel Hill. Several of her books on child development, early education and family literacy are used nationwide. We recommend Dr. Wasik's work as a resource to others.

Then, drawing on a range of research by Wasik and others, we realized that our community had special needs that required a lot of adaptation. PCIL evolved through countless hours of planning, piloting, research and feedback until it reached its current form. At its core, PCIL is an interactive, multi-part series of morning sessions attended by both parents and children, focusing on empowering parents to address the gaps of school readiness in the community. The goals of PCIL are to teach parents the material and skills they need to become their child's first teacher, to coach them as they practice these skills during interactive learning with their child and to build their confidence and awareness through empowerment. We then expect these parents to use their training within the formal PCIL sessions in creative ways, transforming their whole approach to learning in the home.

For the first part of a PCIL session, the parents and their children are separated. While the children are in a different room, receiving a fun warm-up to the topic, the parents are with the main teacher, preparing for the interactive part of the morning session that will follow. This initial period of adults-only preparation in which our teacher helps the parents understand all aspects of the goals for the day – and the goals at home – is an essential facet of our program. See the "Our Resources" section of this book for specific details.

After parents feel comfortable with the content and the activities, parents and their children are brought back together for the second part of the session. Again, you'll find detailed examples in "Our Resources."

For the third part of the session, parents and children are separated for a final time. Children are taken to a different room for structured play and parents exchange feedback with the teacher on challenges and successes they encountered and how they can continue to implement the strategies at home.

PCIL has three key elements that make it successful, as detailed in the color chart at the beginning of this chapter:

- Early Learning Content
- Parent-Child Interaction
- Awareness of the larger importance of early education and goals at home

The Realities We Faced

From Amanda Morgan

When I was brought into this project, I knew right away that English as a Second Language (ESL) for the parents was going to be a very important component of the program if we truly wanted to empower these women and make a real, lasting change using a two-generation approach to school readiness. We wanted to be in the heart of the community so the program was accessible, and it was ideal for us to partner with a school for many reasons. We wanted to have the programming in the school that most of the children would eventually be attending so that they could begin feeling comfortable in that environment. We also wanted to help the parents begin to feel more comfortable interacting with the school and its personnel, in order to build trust and help the parents feel more empowered and engaged in the American school system. We were very grateful for the opportunity to come to Priest Elementary and partner with Detroit Public Schools, because we feel that this was an extremely mutually beneficial relationship for all involved – the school, the community, and ACCESS.

The Detroit Public Schools Office of Adult Education had been running its own ESL class for parents at the school for many years. After I got all of the official approvals to do programming at the school, Nahed's first mission was to start building relationships and see how we could expand and develop the ESL class that existed into a larger ESL program similar to what ACCESS was accustomed to running at our main office, in order to fully meet the needs of the community and serve as the base component for the ACCESS to School Program.

Nahed Alkashbari:

When I arrived at Priest Elementary, the ESL class had about 50 people enrolled, but on many days there were only about 25-30 people who would actually come – a mix of Yemeni and Hispanic women. The ESL teacher faced a big challenge because she was using the cafeteria as a classroom and there was only one level of instruction offered. Everyone was together in one big class, whether they were more advanced learners or they didn't know any English at all. Working in a cafeteria meant that while they were trying to teach in the morning, people were coming and going all the time, preparing for the school's lunchtime. It was loud. We had a lot of challenges right away. Before I could start really working on the program, I knew the first thing we needed to do was divide the class into at least two levels, for more appropriate teaching. We were still in that cafeteria – it's all we had – so we divided the class into two levels, with the two groups facing in two directions and the two of us tried to teach the groups, right there in the cafeteria. We made it work, but it was not easy. I stood at one end of the room, with some learners facing me. The other teacher stood at the other end, with her learners facing her. Of course, we encountered all the kinds of problems you might imagine in such a situation. We both were loud, our voices echoed in the cafeteria, and we each distracted the other's learners. But we did our best. During this time, I was building relationships with people at the school and knew it was time to start looking for other solutions to the challenges and barriers we were seeing.

I went to the principal, and asked if there was any other space in the school. She said at the time, the only space available was the library, so I split the class in half and taught the lower level class in the library. I was able to focus on the material that was more appropriate for their level, and the women began learning at a faster rate.

Amanda Morgan:

We also discovered that the ESL class happening at Priest had not been providing the learners with books because they didn't have the funds. So, we began providing both the lower and higher levels with textbooks and workbooks. The word spread in the community that this was a good place to learn, so enrollment began to increase. As the classes started to expand, and the women began interacting with and trusting Nahed, we began learning about the specific barriers they were facing. It's not that we didn't anticipate some of the barriers we would encounter, but we wanted the program to be structured from what we learned were the actual needs of this community and for their voices to inform our decisions.

Nahed Alkashbari:

The two biggest needs we heard consistently from the women were childcare and transportation. How do the women reach the school in the first place? Yes, we are located in their neighborhood, but even walking a few blocks with children and during our Michigan winters – it's very difficult if you don't own a car or don't have access to the family car. To provide transportation, we hired a driver who used our ACCESS-owned 12-passenger van to drive around the community and pick up people for class. Of course, some of the parents still walked. Some of the parents who drove offered rides to their friends.

The program requires parents to spend time away from home – and that's impossible if there is no one to care for the very young children. So, we also had to address childcare. Many of the women were not used to coming to programming for themselves while they still had young children in the house, so we had to give them a way to bring their young children with them every day. I went to the principal again and asked if there was another room we could use for childcare. She said there were no rooms open. But I couldn't give up that easily. I told her I saw a room that was full of storage items and asked if we could use it if we cleaned it out and found places for everything in the room. She agreed.

Amanda Morgan:

We made sure that the staff we hired to drive our van and work in the childcare room were also immigrant women who spoke the same language as our focus community. We were providing books, childcare and an option for transportation. The classes just kept expanding, so we knew it was time to create more class levels. Again, Nahed went to the principal and asked if there was yet another room we could have. At this point, the principal had witnessed the growth and positive changes that

Important commitments in ACCESS English as a Second Language classes.

had come from us being in the school. Nahed was going to the school's parent meetings to help translate, and we were encouraging the parents to be more involved in the school. This time when Nahed went to the principal and asked for a room, the principal said she would make it happen and we got two classrooms! We then had four ESL classes and the women were split up by levels. We got up to about 120 people enrolled in ESL. We had good attendance rates, and about 60 or so people were on the waiting list at any given time. All the while, we were piloting and adjusting the other three components.

Nahed Alkashbari:

As we moved into classrooms, we only had access to little desks designed for children. I was embarrassed that the women had to try to fit themselves into these tiny desks. This was hard, because at first we didn't have the funds to equip the classrooms at Priest. At ACCESS, our classrooms are fully equipped to provide an environment conducive for learning and we wanted to create that same environment at Priest. When I finally got to this problem, I had to get permission from the principal, so I went to her and said, "We need a bigger size of tables and chairs." I got the OK to move in bigger furniture. So, I set off throughout the school, collecting unused tables and chairs from classrooms, the gym, and storage. Then, we physically moved them. We went through that whole school and we got our classrooms reorganized. Later, ACCESS was able to order new full size tables and chairs for the classrooms. What you see today isn't our original collection of borrowed stuff. We now have new sturdy tables and chairs – the right size for the women.

From Breanne Wainright, coordinator of the English as a Second Language (ESL) program at ACCESS:

I came into the ESL program after Nahed and Amanda had already organized the program, adapted the components in many ways and removed a lot of barriers. I was brought in to coordinate the ESL component so that Nahed and Amanda could really begin focusing on layering in the other three components they had been building and piloting.

We teach ESL using the best practices that teachers in any good program would use, but we are always looking for ways to adjust what we're doing to better meet the needs of these women and to help them learn better and faster. One thing I did was to make up a bright red "English Only Zone" sign, to put up on the wall as a reminder that using their native language should really be a last resort to understanding in the classroom. They should read, write, and speak in English, and if we have tried every other method we can think of to help them understand a concept – acting it out, gestures, pictures, etc. – and they still don't understand, then they can translate for each other. Another thing our Instructors do is write up classroom contracts with each group of learners. They work together to come up with ideas and guidelines that will help the classroom become a productive learning environment. They actually write it on a big piece of paper, then everyone signs it and it is hung on the wall in the classroom.

I see that remarkable, strong commitment made by the parents in the ESL classes. They understand what is at stake. They understand how valuable the program is, how valuable the time with us is – and they are looking for every opportunity to learn. That's why parents from entirely different cultural backgrounds choose to cross the room and sit next to each other. Just saying "hello" and "thank you" to each other is one more chance to learn. Throughout my schooling and training, I've worked with a variety of people from different backgrounds and cultures, but one surprise I've seen over and over again in this program is the willingness of these parents to try whatever we ask of them.

One day, I was teaching a class and had written a paragraph on the white board so that, together as a class, we could find and fix some errors I had included in the text. We talked about concepts like changing the verb tenses in the paragraph. After we had perfected the paragraph, I wanted someone to read the text aloud. The learners knew that it was time to read out loud, and I saw the usual learners getting ready to volunteer. But this time, I said, "Thanks for offering, but is there anyone else who would like to try reading this paragraph?" That's when a couple of other people finally raised their hands. I asked a woman to read, who I wasn't sure was capable of making it all the way through the text. "Would you like to try it?" I asked. Now, think about that situation: We all knew this woman, normally, was shy. She hadn't even volunteered to read, at first. That could be a pretty intimidating situation for this woman. But she didn't shy away. She nodded. And she began.

She read it slowly, word by word. When she got to a word that she wasn't sure how to read, she attempted it and looked right at me. She was wondering: Am I doing it right? And I nodded. She was. Then, she hit a long word – one she just couldn't pronounce correctly. She paused and I could see she wanted me to help her sound it out. So I did. Then the whole class said it with us. And she finally said it herself. And on she went until she had finished the whole paragraph. Can you appreciate how hard that is to accomplish in front of other parents, particularly if you're shy to begin with? But that's how much commitment these parents have to this process. And, each time someone has that kind of experience, all the women in the class grow closer with one another. We are helping to overcome low self-esteem and showing them what a supportive community can do.

Amanda Morgan:

That's the key to this whole process: continually learning, getting feedback, testing what works and making changes in every part of the program. Our challenges on a day- to-day basis were around logistics and removing barriers for the women. But, our greatest challenge overall was designing the content and structure of the Parenting Education and PCIL components.

Take a standard early childhood topic like discipline in the home. Through trial and error, we found the most important questions and perspectives these parents wanted us to address. In more mainstream parenting education classes, you might cover discipline in a pretty standard way. But we find parents start with questions like, "We hear that in America it is illegal to spank your child. Could we go to jail if we spank?" They need us to do a more cross-cultural discussion of expectations for discipline in the home here in America, which might be quite different than in other parts of the world. We have to adapt the topics to the realities of life in our participants' homes.

In PCIL, our goal was helping these parents become their children's first teachers at home. In some ways, you could say the content was obvious for the PCIL component. You know that every early learning class needs to teach shapes and sizes, and the alphabet is the alphabet. But we had to ask: what is the best way to introduce these concepts for this specific community? A lot of programs just assume the parents come in with a full understanding of these concepts, so the facilitators just expect the parents to jump right in and start teaching their children without first teaching the parents the material, demonstrating and having them practice the techniques to work with their children, and helping them become familiar with the activities and materials that many of them had never before used. At ACCESS, we have parents who may struggle with their native alphabet, and are learning the English alphabet for the first time. After trial and error, piloting, focus groups, and working with our evaluators, we found the best way to structure PCIL so that it meets the needs of these parents and accomplishes the goals we set out.

Nahed Alkashbari:

Some early childhood programs might start a session with the parents and their children in the same room. We begin our PCIL sessions with the parents in a classroom with me, while their children are getting a start on the day's lessons in a different classroom, in a fun way with games, songs and other activities. This also gives the children time to work off some of their energy. They're not always quite ready to sit down and pay attention to the things their parents will show them, sitting at tables together in our classroom. So, in their own separate room, the children can learn by singing, or even dancing. Or the teacher might say, "Stomp three times! One! Two! Three!" Children love to stomp. Or, "Find the 'A' on the floor mat!" And they love to run over and show us the "A." By giving the parents time with me in a separate room, without any distractions, they can concentrate on all the steps I'm showing them for engaging later with their children. At the end of the morning PCIL sessions we also discovered that we needed to give the parents more time with me, without their children, so they could ask questions and give feedback. And I can encourage them and give them feedback, too. When we do it this way, they usually have a lot of questions that make a big difference in how they carry out these lessons at home.

Once we perfected this basic organization of the PCIL component, we did discover more surprises. For example, in the beginning, the first time we placed the children in a separate room to start the morning session, some of the children were still so attached to their parents that they wouldn't even remain in the children's classroom. Once again, we had to adjust. Sometimes, a mother stays with her children for a couple of weeks. Other times, we are able to help the mothers make the transition right away. We do find that, quite soon, the mothers tell me, "My child now says he wants to go to school!" Or, "Now, my child asks, 'When can we go see Miss Nahed again?'" We help them make this transition. That is one important step in school readiness. Another surprise is how much these parents are learning in our sessions. You might think that all parents understand the topics we cover, so we might be doing more of a review. But that's not the case. I'm often teaching something, like how to shape a letter, what strokes you use to make an "M," for example. And I will hear, "Oh, I didn't know that!" When I check back in on our step-by-step approach, at a later session, I'll hear from mothers who are doing one letter each day. "What letter are you on today?" I might ask. And they'll know. They'll tell me something like, "We're doing "S" today!" I emphasize that they should work at whatever pace is appropriate for their child and their home. Some move faster than others. By discussing it this way, and voicing feedback in the group of parents, it also shows other mothers in the group: Oh, look, all the other women are doing this in their homes. Hmmm, I'm going to keep going with this myself.

One of the larger goals in the program is establishing expectations and routines. Children crave a routine. We talk about this throughout ACCESS to School's components for parents. Let's take an expectation like establishing an earlier bedtime for younger children. Some families don't have a cultural expectation about this. I've seen parents in the supermarkets at 10 or 11 p.m. with their little children in their carts as they shop. From the mother's perspective, this might be the first moment in her day that she feels she is free to go do this shopping, but in the parenting classes we talk about how younger children need more sleep. We teach other structures in a family routine they can establish at home. One example is: Brush your teeth before you go to bed. It's a step you can always take before you hop into bed. Some families don't have a structure like that until we encourage it. Or: Read to your children before bed. Some homes don't have any books. We may be providing the first reading materials in some homes.

There is a balance we need in this approach to parents. Many of these mothers have a lot of fears in this new country. In their old home, they might have let their children run freely through the whole village. Here, in the middle of a big city, they may fear what will happen to their children if they let them play outside. In our program, we show them all of these things parents can do to help their children succeed in school. This can make some parents feel even more burdened. It can add to their low self-esteem. Some of them have lived here for a while but are fearful about some things. They may even have trouble talking about their children's condition with their doctor, which can result in a mindset of low self-esteem. We have to be careful to be sure we are helping to build them up, not adding to the problem. We have to emphasize to them that, as parents, they are the ones who lead and supervise and guide the family. Let's say a parent can't speak enough English to talk to the doctor, or someone at a store, so they fall into the practice of having the children translate for them. This can become a pattern of letting the child lead. We try to open the parents' eyes to what is happening. As we teach them new skills, we keep reminding them that they are the ones in charge in the home. That's why so many of our parents take this program very seriously. They know they are here to learn and they understand what is at stake for their families. And, very soon, if they follow the lessons we are teaching, they make a discovery. A mother will come to me and say, "Wow! My child and I are now so much closer together." One of our biggest challenges is simply overcoming that feeling many immigrant parents have in questioning their own worth; questioning their own abilities. They have to overcome a pattern of doubting themselves.

Lessons Learned

From Amanda Morgan:

Working with the Social Innovation Fund means that we rigorously research and evaluate everything we do. This is an ongoing process, and it holds us to high standards. One of the first phases in this process was a full year of implementation evaluation, which included pilot-testing, compliance reviews, focus groups and interviews with staff and participants. All of this information was analyzed and used to improve our work. If you are reading our book with the goal of developing or improving your own program, it is important to note that our success in this long process of developing ACCESS to School is a result of our strong commitment to evaluating everything we were doing and using this information to improve the program and our delivery.

Some of our Tips for Success can be found throughout the book. Below are a few more examples of lessons learned collected by our team:

Building a Strong Partnership with the Schools –

As we have mentioned earlier, we felt that having our program in the school was the most beneficial place for the parents and their children, and it also benefits the school. As a trusted community-based agency, we were able to build bridges between the school and the community. For the parents who were new to the school, we were able to introduce them to this environment and get them comfortable, and for parents whose older children were already attending Priest Elementary, we were able to increase their engagement in the school. One lesson we have learned at ACCESS, which was reinforced in this new program, is that school officials get a constant stream of requests from entities offering programs and partnerships. But, many of these ideas never get off the ground, others don't last long, and some prove to have little value. Officials often become wary about accepting such proposals. For good reason, they are careful about agreeing to new partnerships. If you are looking to build a strong partnership with a school, make sure you are willing to show them that the partnership will be mutually beneficial. Think about the unique skills and resources your agency can offer to bring to the school beyond the scope of your specific program. For example, at ACCESS, we offer to send staff to translate/interpret in Arabic for the school staff in settings such as parent/teacher conferences. It may not be directly related to the program, but it's a way to build a strong partnership and let the school know that you are committed to them and the families that you both serve.

The Importance of Case Management –

ACCESS believes that we must work with the whole person in the context of their family and community if we truly want the person to reach their fullest potential. ACCESS has multiple sites in the region that provide social services, many programs that include case management components, and the whole agency embraces the wrap-around services model so clients' needs are always being addressed.

In the ACCESS to School Program, we knew from the beginning that although we didn't have the capacity to actually provide the many services the women would need on site, having a case management component helped to address the needs and barriers that were present, through resources, guidance and referrals. It helped the women navigate the systems they often struggled with, helped them become more empowered as individuals and parents, and helped them meet their basic needs. The case management component was the key to retention, as we were able to monitor the progress of the learners and help them remove barriers before they dropped out of our program. We also found that by setting goals with the women during case management, they took more ownership over the program and their learning.

Building a Strengths-Based Program with Empowerment as the Goal –

It's easy to get overwhelmed on a daily basis and it can be tempting to apply one's own expectations and perspectives to a situation and see only the barriers and challenges. But, it's important to make sure that your team takes time to remind itself of the strengths of the community. It's easy to see the values, commitment, humility, generosity, and kindness of our focus community without having to look hard. The more you get to know the community, the more strengths you will uncover, and the approach you take should be strengths-based, rather than deficits-based. Focus on structuring a program that will build on what the participants are already good at so you are honoring their dignity and they are being successful from the beginning.

We have many outcomes and goals in our ACCESS to School Program. The primary goal – the goal that we always went back to when we were making decisions and reminding ourselves of our priorities – was always empowerment. When empowerment is kept at the forefront of every decision, from the way you structure the classes to the curriculum you choose, it provides the foundation for all of the other goals and outcomes to be reached. We felt that in order for us to make lasting change in these children's lives and in the community at large, we always needed to be working toward the mothers feeling empowered. If, through this process of learning new skills, they recognized their own skills and abilities and began to build their self-esteem, they could more easily take on this role of first teacher of their child. Learning and applying the material is the easier part.

Developing a Comprehensive Message to Participants –

During the first year of ACCESS to School, we commonly talked to participants about the four program components separately. We referred to ESL, Parenting Education, Case Management and PCIL distinctly, and discussed scheduling issues for each one separately. Our attendance rates already were improving and had reached a fair level–but we knew we could do better. We investigated the reasons for dips in attendance. Quite a few reasons surfaced, but the two that pertained to the schedule were: 1.) The classes were happening on different days and times and participants didn't want to stay and wait or return for their next class; and, 2.) Some participants didn't realize that the components were all a part of an interconnected program and thought they could choose whichever ones they wanted to attend and skip the others. In our second year, we started marketing ACCESS to School as one comprehensive program, so instead of telling parents at registration that they were in all the specific classes, we talked about what it meant to be enrolled in the ACCESS to School Program as a whole. We also shifted our schedule. For example, we moved the Parenting Education class so that it was in the hour between the two ESL class times, so that none of the participants would have to wait or come back to attend Parenting Education.

Finding the Right Parenting Curriculum –

As you have seen in this chapter, one of our biggest challenges was finding a successful Parenting Education curriculum that would work effectively in our community. Off-the-shelf curricula that we explored quickly met resistance. Some of the topics seemed irrelevant: the teaching perspectives made assumptions that were foreign to these parents' living situations. One example is the level of privacy our families expected when discussing parenting issues. In American culture, many adults are very open about sharing intimate issues in the home. Our parents have a different cultural expectation: Their families expect to maintain more privacy about family matters. Although the women prefer native English-speaking Americans to teach the ESL classes, the parenting teacher must be a trusted member of our community who is skilled as a facilitator, speaks their native language and genuinely cares about making participants feel comfortable and safe. Another example of adjustment is that mainstream curricula tend to quickly cover broad topics in a concise number of sessions. After all, parents are busy and it's common to try to move as fast as possible. However, we found that we needed to move our parents through the topics over a greater number of weeks, to provide for a slower process of teaching, review and feedback.

Evaluation and data collection –

ACCESS has always seen the value of evaluation, not only to measure progress towards our outcomes, but also to use that information to improve our programs. The SIF's rigorous evaluation standards gave us an opportunity to plan ahead and think critically about what a good evaluation in this community should look like. We started out looking for standardized school readiness and parent assessments (relating to stress, self-efficacy, activities in the home, etc.) that had been formed for this community and could not find any. We then looked for standardized assessments that measured our outcomes and began a long process of breaking down each assessment, question by question, analyzing whether or not the community would understand the meaning, the context, and the wording. We changed questions we felt would be problematic, ensuring they still got at the same information. Then, we translated and back-translated each question and conducted pilot testing for all the questions, with follow-up interviews. Finally, we adjusted the questions that showed consistent problems or confusion one last time.

For all of the parent outcomes, we have survey questions that use a Likert scale (options ranging from strongly disagree to strongly agree). In America, this concept of choosing an answer on a scale of how much we agree with a statement is common, as we are taught how to do this from a young age. But this scale is initially difficult for these women to understand because most, if not all, of them have not ever used this type of scale before. We had to create practice questions at the beginning of the survey so that after Nahed thoroughly explained the scale to them, she could have them take the practice questions to make sure they understood how the scale worked. Even then, the women would often get frustrated and say, "Why can't I just answer 'yes' or 'no'?". These barriers add complexities to data collection, and if not monitored, can cause inaccurate data.

Although we had independent evaluators for this project, we chose to have our program staff administer the surveys and collect the data for many reasons. This process is labor intensive and time consuming, but we felt there were many more benefits that outweighed these issues. First, trust and comfort was a big concern for the women in our program. We knew from the beginning that our data collection process would not be successful if we had "outsiders" come in and try to discuss sensitive parenting topics with this community. Second, even though the surveys were translated in Arabic and Spanish, some of the women had difficulty reading in their native language, so we needed someone who could sit with them and read each question. Lastly, having staff involved in the evaluation process from the beginning created meaningful buy-in from the staff and the evaluation process became an integrated and important part of the program, rather than an auxiliary piece that is looked at in the end.

We recognize that we had a unique opportunity to have the time and funds to complete an implementation evaluation, and be able to plan, monitor, and adjust our programming. We hope that what you take away from this is not that in order to be successful you must do all of these activities as well, but rather, through this book, you can learn from this information and apply it where applicable to your own agencies, programs, jobs and communities.

Layla Assofe's picture of her school.

Voices of Our Families

In this chapter of the book, you will meet some of the families whose lives have been shaped by ACCESS to School. One day, we invited parents who had completed the Parent and Child Interactive Learning component of our program to come to a Priest Elementary School classroom and talk with us about their experiences in the program – and, later, in their homes. We invited their children to come with them and asked the kids to draw pictures of the topics we were discussing.

Layla Assofe, 4, was born in Yemen and came to this country two years ago. Her photo is on the cover of this book. Layla and her mom have been learning English and basic literacy concepts through ACCESS to School, and particularly in the 10-week Interactive Learning program. One of the first goals of this program is to calm immigrant families' fears about going to their local schools and engaging in classrooms where the teachers and the language seem so foreign to them.

We all talked around a table while the children were asked to draw pictures. Layla chose a seat across the table from Khalil Assofe, a 4-year-old cousin who also had been born in Yemen but came to the U.S. only six months ago. We asked the kids, "Can you draw a picture of your school? You know – this place, Priest School, where you come for classes with your mom? Can you draw your school?"

Layla's cousin paused. He selected a red marker and began painstakingly working on a rectangular shape – trying to represent the building.

But before his marker had ever touched the paper, Layla was already at work – her eyes searching the classroom. Why? She spotted her teacher, Nahed Alkashbari, and carefully selected a brown marker about the same color as the *hijab*, the traditional Muslim headscarf, that her teacher was wearing that day. Layla used the marker to draw her teacher. "Miss Nahed," she said as she drew.

That was just the beginning for Layla. When her picture of Miss Nahed was finished, she smiled up at us from the white paper, looking around the room again and choosing another color that matched clothing worn by a classroom helper. One more figure soon stood next to Layla's depiction of Miss Nahed, arms outstretched and welcoming. A third figure soon followed, and then a fourth. Four of the adults who were helping in the classroom soon stretched across the paper – all smiling, all welcoming.

Layla's younger cousin was working on his respectable rectangular sketch of the school. He understood the question in a concrete way: Draw the building. Instead, Layla had drawn the people who fill her classroom.

"This is my school!" Layla proudly pointed her marker and one colorfully ink-stained index finger at Miss Nahed, and then swept that gesture around the room. "All of you – my school."

> ### Tip for Success: Education Starts on Day 1
> Children who live in healthy, vibrant communities that offer rich learning opportunities have a better chance of entering kindergarten prepared, which sets them on the path for lifelong success. In Michigan, 1 in 4 kids lives in poverty; roughly half of these children live in families in extreme poverty, with annual incomes below $10,000. Fewer than half of children living in poverty are ready for school at age 5.
> Source: United Way for Southeastern Michigan

All of the children we interviewed that day were enthusiastic as they pulled up a chair, dumped the colored markers out of their box and onto the table, and tackled whatever sketches were requested. They were right at home – and eager to show off their learning.

"Can you draw a picture of you and your mother?" we asked 4-year-old Ra'ed Yahya. Thoraya Alhaggam, an immigrant from rural Yemen, was wearing a blue *hijab* – so Ra'ed selected a blue marker and began his drawing with a practiced up-and-down curve. That confidently sketched curve on his paper was the basic shape of his mother's *hijab*-covered head and shoulders. Then Ra'ed added big, bright eyes and a smile.

"Oh my!" His mother laughed and smiled down over his shoulder. "Yes, it's me."

"That's wonderful," Nahed said. The boy was still drawing, quickly sketching himself to the right of his mother and squiggling the marker across the top of his head. "Oh, you even got your haircut there!" Nahed told him.

Ra'ed's marker moved on to form a symbol between them. "That's a heart," his mother said, proudly identifying the shape. "Look at that."

Ra'ed was enjoying the praise for this exhibition of his skills. "Now, let me show you my sister, Rayah." Soon, Rayah's face joined them on the left side of the paper – and his marker quickly sketched a couple more hearts.

"He's full of love," Nahed said.

As Ra'ed felt confidence in completing his sketch, he began speaking in full English sentences to the adults around him. "I even know how to draw playing soccer." We asked him to show us. On a new piece of paper, another marker soon was forming a ball, then a brown oval near the ball. "Now I'm drawing my big feet as I run up and kick it very hard – I can kick it way up in the air." Using more markers, he managed to squeeze his whole body onto the paper, drawing upward from his brown feet. "And now I'm drawing my face, my eyes." Ra'ed looked at Nahed and recalled that earlier comment about his hair. "Oh, and my hair! Here's how my hair looks." A few squiggles and the hair was perfect.

Soon, Ra'ed was drawing his favorite foods, starting with an orange. He had a blue marker in his hand, so the basic circle shape of the orange turned out blue. "Oh!" he said in exasperation, and reached for the orange marker. He had spotted his error. "It's orange!" he sighed, the new marker in his hand. He filled in the blue circle to make it look like a real orange.

Ra'ed Yahya draws his Mom, himself and his sister.

"Can you write your name – to take credit for all of this work?" we asked.

"Yes!" Pulling up a fresh piece of paper, Ra'ed chose a green marker and boldly filled the 8-by-11 paper with a perfectly formed: "Ra'ed."

His mother, Thoraya, explained: "When he first came to Priest to study with me, he didn't know how to write his name. Now he loves to write his name. This has helped us a lot. When we come here, they teach how to be self-esteem. Sorry, I still don't speak perfect English, but you know – but how to have self-esteem. Right? How to build up self-esteem. They teach the children how to be responsible for themselves, and how to behave with others in the community outside.”

“Why is that so important?” we asked.

“Here, we live in this big city, but we come – our family comes from the country,” Thoraya explained. “When we used to live in the country, things were different for kids. Freer – more free for kids. They could just go out and be free. But when we come here, for the safety, you know, we spent most time in the house. Too much time in the house!” she sighed. “But it wasn’t safe for the kids to go outside like it was back when we were in the country where we lived before. So, too much time in the house – you know what it means? Means kids can get to fighting and arguing. But when we do this – he loves it. He loves being with me. We come and we study. We learn. And there’s fun, too, yes. But we know it’s to study, first. We learn a lot by doing this. Numbers. Colors. Shapes. Letters.”

Taking a cue from Mom to ensure that we all knew that he could write more than the four letters of his name, Ra’ed began writing all 26 letters – in order. As he drew, he said, “That’s A.” Then, “That’s B.” Occasionally, he would pause and recite the whole series he had written, singing the letters to the popular alphabet tune known by millions of kids nationwide.

He also pointed out, “I can write the numbers now, too.” When he didn’t get an immediate request for that, he suggested other sketches. “I can draw a snake, too. Want a snake? Or I can draw a fast car – vroom! Boom. Vroom!”

And that reminded Thoraya of a rhyming game that had proven a big hit after Miss Nahed had taught it to the parents and children. “Oh, that rhyming. He loves it. We take what we learn here and go home with it. And now Ra’ed and Rayah – it’s rhyming game even when I’m not with them.”

“How does the rhyming game go?” we asked Ra’ed.

He smiled. “Bed!” he shouted. Then, he pointed toward his nose. “Head!” And he looked around the room for a moment. “Something red!”

“That’s it,” his mother said. “He and Rayah run around the house – try to find the things. And sometimes they come to see me to ask if something is right. Does this word rhyme? Is it right?"

"That's one of the activities I give them to take home and keep going with their learning," Nahed said. "There are many of these activities through the program. I give them study sheets to use at home. I give them activities to do with shapes and numbers and all the rest."

"Numbers and letters," Thoraya said. "Oh, we sing about them!"

Thoraya paused for a moment. "You know, the first day Ra'ed came to study here, he did not even want to hold a pen. Maybe he didn't know how. But he didn't hold it – wouldn't hold it." Clearly, from her expression as she said this, she was embarrassed by that first moment with her son. Then, she brightened and nodded confidently: "But now? Now he's had so much self-esteem for this. Now, at our house: No more, 'I don't want to go to school!' He is crying: 'When do we go to school?'"

> **The High Cost of Ignoring School Readiness.**
> According to Brookings Institution, children not kindergarten-ready are half as likely to read well by third grade. According to America's Promise Alliance, children not reading proficiently by third grade are four times more likely to drop out before finishing high school.

Most of the families in ACCESS to School are Yemeni-American. One of the surprises in the program's first couple of years was the rising need for successful blending with a minority of Hispanic mothers and their children.

"I did not know what would happen," said Nahed Alkashbari. "But we began to have interest in the program from some of the Hispanic parents in the area, so we had both groups in parenting classes and in the Parent and Child Interactive Learning component. I wondered if the ladies would separate themselves – I thought that might happen. But, instead, they enjoyed meeting each other and they started teaching each other some of their own languages – as well as the English I was teaching. I was so pleased to see that."

Candelaria Ansorena, who was born in Mexico and migrated to the United States in 1998, says she was firmly set on a personal mission when she first met Nahed through the English as a Second Language program at Priest. After years of isolation due to her inability to speak clear English and lack of a high school diploma, Candelaria found an opportunity when she realized that she was close to having all three of her children at school age. As she began to think about having all three kids out of the house during the school year, she decided that it was her time to study, learn English and pass a high school equivalency test. Plus, as her youngest son neared school age, she was determined that he would get as strong a start as possible at Priest. ACCESS to School was a doorway to all of her hopes, she said.

"Once I started with ESL classes, and then I finished my first level of English – that made me want to finish all the levels. I am doing all I can. I have started GED classes. I live near the school here, so I can be here every day. I don't miss," she said.

Through the ESL classes, Candelaria found out about the parenting classes, and her son was the right age for the Interactive Learning component, as well, in early 2015. "I wanted my son to be successful when he started school, so I liked that he could be with me in this with Nahed," she said.

We asked, "What did you think when you first met Nahed – wearing a *hijab* and clearly from a much different part of the world than your own family?"

"Only one thing matters to me: I want to help my kids to learn. And, I want to do anything that can help make our lives better. I don't care who the person is running things. I don't think I even stopped to think about the *hijab* she was wearing. When I met Nahed and began going to her classes, I could tell that she was a very nice, friendly person who explained things she was teaching us very clearly. She's a very good teacher. And my son, now here in 2016 – he is in school here at Priest. He remembers Nahed, and asks about her. 'When are we going to see Miss Nahed again?' He really liked being in the program."

"What about the other moms you met in the program?" we asked. "Some of them are only starting to learn English – and they don't know Spanish – and they're from a different culture than Mexico. Any difficulty making friends?"

"No! We learn from each other," Candelaria said. "I know how to say hello – a greeting: '*As-salamu alaykum*' – Peace be with you. And we like to say '*masha'Allah*'. That's like saying, 'It's good news!' We say that to each other when something good has happened."

"And in Spanish?" we asked.

"Oh, they learned some Spanish. They like to greet us now, '*Como estas!*' And you know, we say, '*Bien, gracias.*' I even know, now, when someone is asking me, 'Where's the *baño*?' You know, the bathroom. When we come to class, I always like to sit with someone who can teach me something. I am coming to learn. I don't miss any of the classes; this is so important to me. So, all the time: *How can I do more to make our lives better? How can I learn? How can my son learn?* I learn from Nahed. I learn from the other ladies. That is what I want."

That's why, Candelaria said, she most appreciates Nahed's focus in the Interactive Learning sessions on explaining to parents strategies they can use at home.

"It's OK to learn here, but what about after? How am I going to get my son to do these things at home? How am I going to get him learning about letters and numbers and shapes and all these things – at home? This is the question," Candelaria said. "And Nahed has taught us these ways – these things – these strategies. Here is the problem: At first, he did not want to count or play with letters at home. Oh, no! Not that. But Nahed showed us how to get him learning – and I remember all the things she taught us. I remember because I use them."

"Like what?" we asked.

"Shapes," she said. "Shapes are all over the house. We find them everywhere. Like in the kitchen, we find a triangle and a circle. A box in the kitchen – is it a square or is it a rectangle? And in other rooms? A light switch. Think! There is a light switch in every room. And what is the shape we see? A rectangle. Now, as we go through the house, we are learning."

Then, she turned to Nahed and added, "Or the – the cards… "

"Oh, the flash cards," Nahed said. "We show the parents how to use flash cards for everything from numbers and letters to … "

"Yes, the flash cards!" Candelaria said. "Those really work. Yes, we use them at home, too. I don't forget what Nahed taught us. I remember all the things we learned."

Candelaria is so committed to the program that she volunteered to keep coming to classes even after she and her son finished their Interactive Learning series in early 2015. Her youngest son began regular classes at Priest in the fall of 2016, and Candelaria returned to the classroom to help Nahed with any English-Spanish translation issues that might arise in the next classes Nahed was teaching.

"Why am I doing this? Why?" Candelaria asked. "Well, it is like this: It is smart to help. I need to keep using my lessons so that I keep learning. One way to do that is to help others learn. That keeps me reviewing everything I learn. Last year, after our parenting classes with my son were over, I kept coming every day to help. Now, I see my youngest son – he has started school strong. His teacher told me that, when he started at Priest, he knew all the things they want children to know. And now it's my time to keep learning so that I can help my children keep learning – and so that I can find good work someday. I have worked cleaning houses, but I want to do other work. So, this program – it showed me new ways to learn, new ways to teach my children – and it keeps me learning and practicing with them even when we are at home."

Some children were quieter than others. Some preferred to let their drawings speak for them. Others enjoyed simply making concrete responses to the queries for pictures.

Khalil Assofe, 4, was just getting over a cold and was eager to break open his marker box and start drawing – but he didn't talk as expressively about his sketches as his cousin, Layla, had. He demonstrated that he could write his name in big, colorful block letters. He drew shapes: stars, hearts, triangles and squares.

"Tell us about these shapes?" we asked, in attempts to get him talking.

He pointed. "This is a triangle. This is a star."

After such precision in many of his sketches, we noticed that Khalil was drawing what appeared to be a less-than-circular circle. The lines narrowed around the middle.

"And is that your circle?" we asked.

"No," he replied in a soft, matter-of-fact voice. "It's an oval."

Khalil's mom explained, "He would talk more, but he doesn't feel too good today."

During our time together, Khalil remained a boy of many images but few words.

"Why do you like to come to school with your mom?" we asked, hoping to get him talking about feelings toward the school – and his mom's participation with him.

But he had nothing to say.

We turned back to images and asked him to trace hands. Once again, the question turned into a colorful sketch. He selected a pink marker and carefully traced around his mother's hand on a piece of paper. Then, over the top of that pink outline, he placed his own hand. In yellow, he traced his own, smaller fingers, intertwined with hers.

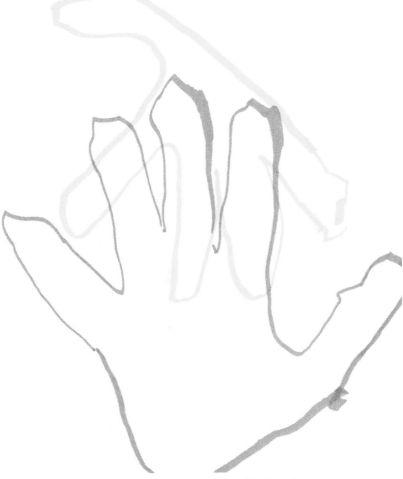

Khalil draws his Mom and his hand.

*Nahed Alkashbari starts the PCIL morning
with Yemeni-American mothers.*

Our Day at School

"Good morning!" Nahed Alkashbari calls cheerily to a circle of Yemeni-American women in a classroom at Priest Elementary School. It is precisely 9 a.m. on a Friday morning.

Collectively, the women call back, "Good morning!"

Welcome to a typical morning in the most distinctive of the four components in ACCESS to School: the once-a-week Parent and Child Interactive Learning (PCIL) session. We are showing you this particular morning session, documented through recordings, to capture the details as they unfold – because this time, Nahed Alkashbari and the ACCESS support team are working with a group of recent immigrants from Yemen. This group of mothers recently started the ACCESS English as a Second Language (ESL) classes, and when they enrolled in ESL, our staff identified that they have children between the ages 3 and 5 – therefore qualifying them for the PCIL component of our program. (See the "Our Story" chapter for more details about how these four components work together.) During the 10-week PCIL series, parents learn the importance of acting as their children's first teachers while the youngsters are still at home. These 10 PCIL sessions also introduce the parents to subject matter and interactive techniques that they can use to meet goals as early educators long after the PCIL classes end. By following these mothers and their children through a typical morning at PCIL, you will see how quickly even recent immigrants with limited English language skills begin to understand and start working on the larger goal of school readiness.

This group of parents and children gathers at Priest Elementary School before the 9 a.m. session begins, so the children can be dropped off in a room just a few doors away from the parents-only classroom. After several weeks of these PCIL sessions, all but one of the youngsters eagerly join the other children for games, learning and a snack, letting the mothers head off toward their own classroom. One boy hesitates at the door of the children's classroom, refusing to drop his mother's hand, shaking his head and talking urgently in Arabic phrases. There's so much anxiety that his mother agrees to go with him into the children's room. She moves to one side of the classroom and, as her son continues to eye her sitting along one wall, he begins stepping toward the other children. The staff reassures the mother that this is fine; nothing for her to be anxious about at this point. She settles into her seat and resolves to stay just one more week in the children's room to reassure her son.

In the parents' room, Nahed greets the other mothers at 9 a.m. and then immediately asks, "How are your kids today?" Then she changes up the question to use a different noun: "How are your *children* today?"

One mother replies, "They were happy to come here today."

Says another: "No problem today."

A third: "Happy today." Then, "We are happy today to go to school."

Several others answer in Arabic, as Nahed nods and responds. Clearly, all of these mothers are proud that their children are now eager to attend school with them – and that they have conquered separation anxiety, at least for these morning sessions.

"That's how it should be," Nahed responds. "Yes. Good. We've got just one more to go," she says, referring to the one mother still in the children's room. "So, this is good."

A U-shaped arrangement of tables fills most of the parents' classroom, as do cupboards and file cabinets packed with educational supplies. The walls are lined with colorful charts and bulletin boards, reminding parents about letters, numbers, key terms and the upcoming schedule. At one corner of the U-shaped table arrangement, Nahed has lined up samples of all the materials the parents soon will be using in the interactive session with their children. Nahed also has a laptop, speakers and a projector set up on a table in the middle of the U for media clips of the day's subject: the letters M(m), N(n), O(o), P(p), Q(q) and R(r).

"Today we are going to continue with the alphabet. Can anyone tell me: What did we study in our last two classes?" Nahed asks, holding up two fingers as she says the phrase, "last two classes." Then she asks, "Who can tell me what part of the alphabet we studied in the last two classes?" Waving backward over her shoulder and holding up two fingers, Nahed is visually underscoring the meaning of key words.

"The start of the alphabet," answers one woman, in English. Others respond at the same time, in Arabic. "In English," Nahed urges, and one woman uses English to explain the letters covered in the last two classes.

"Yes, that's right. So let's say the letters together now," Nahed says. In unison, the mothers begin clearly and precisely reciting, "A, B, C … " through the letter "L." Nahed then leads the entire recitation a second time, pointing to each letter in turn on a wall chart. "Yes, these were the letters in our last two classes, right?"

"Yes, in our last two classes," repeats one of the mothers, in English.

"Today, we are learning about the language and thinking development of our children – for your children and for all children at this age. Do you understand this?" Nahed asks, taking a question for clarification in Arabic from one mother. Nahed listens for a moment, then nods, and in English, says, "It's OK. Yes, I will repeat what I have just said so we all understand. Today, we are learning about *language*" – and her hand moves outward from her mouth to visualize the concept – "and *thinking*" – and her finger points to her head. She repeats the words and the motions. "And this is for all children. By 3 years old, children should be saying complete sentences – complete sentences."

The mothers nod, then Nahed asks them, "What is a complete sentence?" Several mothers respond in Arabic, explaining the concept. Nahed confirms what they are saying. "Yes, that is what we mean by a complete sentence. Who can give me a complete sentence – in English, this time?"

One woman says, "My boy likes to go to school."

"Yes!" Nahed says, all the time using vivid hand motions and enunciating precisely as she speaks. "Yes. And at about this age, by about 3, children are using complete sentences. And we don't mean just two-word phrases; we are talking about complete sentences using more of the new words they are learning every day. By 4, their sentences will be even longer."

She takes a quick question in Arabic from one mother and responds, "Let's talk about this. So, does every child do this at exactly the same time? No, they don't. Children are different. But at about age 3, you should be looking for your children to speak in complete sentences. Do I mean on their birthday when they turn 3? No, I mean that at about age 3 – *about* age 3 – you should be hearing complete sentences, and those sentences will get longer as they reach age 4. And their vocabulary – their vocabulary, the number of words they know, their vocabulary – will grow until they know more than 1,500 words. That's 1,500 words – so many words, right? Remember when they knew just a handful of words, when they were younger? Now they are learning so many words – they are building up their vocabulary, their *vocabulary*. And, of course, they don't stop at 1,500 words. They are learning new words every day. So they know even more than the 1,500 words when they are about 4 years old – *about* 4 years old. Many words! And these "many" words they are learning from their growing vocabulary."

Nahed pauses and looks carefully at the faces around her. "So, now a question. As parents, as we watch our children develop, as we watch their *language* and their *thinking* develop, what are we looking for?" she asks. "We are looking for … "

"Sentences," says one mother. "Sentences and vocabulary."

"Yes. Do we all understand this?" She sees nods, and several mothers respond briefly in Arabic. "Yes," Nahed says, and nods. "Yes, very good."

"And how do we know that, at this age, our children are going through this development in thinking and language? How do we know?" she asks.

One woman answers in Arabic, conveying a point Nahed has made for several weeks: Parents need to take time to sit down and talk with their children.

"Yes, very good!" Nahed says. "Yes, do we all understand that? In English, now: We must take time to listen – to listen to our children – and to talk with our children. And this is easy, if we take the time, because we are seeing that these children now have so many questions – questions they are eager to ask us," Nahed explains. "Perhaps *too many* questions, right?"

The mothers chuckle.

"Now, if they are so eager to talk to us, why don't we sit down and spend more time talking and listening? Why might we forget to do this?" Nahed asks, and several mothers respond briefly in Arabic. "Yes," she says at length. "Yes, we are so busy aren't we? We are so busy with cooking and cleaning and taking care of things around the house. We may not feel we have this time. But we cannot just give up on this, can we? We must find the time. We make the time because we know that talking with our children and listening to our children helps them to prepare for school. If you can't sit and talk right at the minute your child asks you a question, you can plan for a time – perhaps right after dinner, or perhaps some other time. We should plan for this time each day."

Nahed then reviews several developmental milestones that she has covered in past classes, and repeats her point about paying attention to vocabulary and sentences. She briefly touches on several more milestones that she will discuss more fully in the future. One concept Nahed introduces this morning is the matching of pictures and objects, which is an early step in a child's ability to match tangible things they encounter in the real world with the abstract representation of a picture. The developmental process of visual discrimination leads to a child's ability to sort, classify and eventually read and do math, Nahed explains, using her hands and repeating as she goes. "So, when we are working with our children and we ask them to match a picture to an object, this is an important developmental skill.

This is a good thing to do. Matching – asking your child to work with you on matching – helps them to learn."

She asks if everyone understands this concept, then exchanges a few questions and answers in Arabic with the mothers.

Tip for Success: Patience, Repetition and Review

Parents in our full ACCESS to School Program – including the PCIL component – have a range of abilities with the English language and a wide range of experiences with formal education. The parents in the morning PCIL session we are showcasing in this chapter are just beginning to learn English, and most had little opportunity for formal education when they were growing up in Yemen. If you are developing a similar program, remember that introducing a seemingly common activity – like drawing a line between "matching" images on a worksheet – may be a first-time concept for some parents. Even our overall goal of helping parents to understand that learning begins at birth sometimes takes time for parents to embrace. While ACCESS participants value education, many of them come from a culture where education is equated with enrollment in school. Among our core values in this safe learning community are patience, repetition and review, along with plenty of planning for extra opportunities to clearly explain the concepts being introduced each week.

Nahed glances at the clock. "We only have so much time here – until 9:45," she reminds the mothers. "So, let's turn to the new alphabet letters you will be working with this morning when you and your children sit down together. But first, let's review how we introduce new letters. What are the key words we need to know as we teach the letters? Let's go over the key words."

With a dry-erase marker in her hand, Nahed asks the group, "What do we do first when introducing the letters? We – ? "

"Name the letter," answers one mother.

Nahed writes the word "Name" on the board. "Yes, first we *name* the letter. And remember, naming the letter is different than the letter's *sound*. So first, we *name* the letter. And what are the names of our letters for this week?"

She leads a recitation of "M," "N," "O," "P," "Q," and "R." She hears varying pronunciations of "Q," so she goes back to that letter, and for a full minute, they practice saying "Q."

"As we name the letters, we want to help our children by pointing to the letters we see. We *point*," Nahed says, taping a big sketch of a hand with one finger pointing onto the white board beneath the word "Name." Nahed then points at each letter on the white board and repeats, "We *name* the letters. We *point* to the letters. And then we – ? "

"Sound the letter," says a mother.

Nahed writes the word "Sound" on the board and reviews the concept. She clicks on her laptop computer and plays audio of various male and female voices sounding each of the six letters. As a group, the women practice the sounds of the six letters, then they review the name of each letter compared with the sound. "The name of this letter is *em*," Nahed says, pointing to the "M," and repeats, "em, em. That's the name of M. And what is the sound of this letter, 'M?' It is *mmm, mmm*."

After reviewing all six letters, Nahed asks for the fourth key term they will use in teaching letters. "Next, we trace. *Trace*. We help our children to trace the letters."

Summing up the lesson, Nahed says, "Now, let's say I'm going to teach the letter 'M' to my child today. We begin by naming the letter 'M.' We point to the letter 'M' in front of us on our paper, or in a workbook or on the magnet board. We sound the letter 'M.' We use one of our worksheets to trace the letter 'M.'"

She distributes a series of worksheets that cover each of the morning's six letters. Then, she asks the mothers to turn toward each other, in pairs, as she demonstrates how to use each worksheet – including sheets with small arrows showing how to take a fingertip or crayon and properly trace the shape of the letter.

"And what else can I say about the letter 'M?'" Nahed asks.

"'M' is for 'mouse,'" says a parent.

"More words!"

They call out, "Milk!" "Mom!" "Money!" "Monkey!" "Moon!"

Nahed then moves on to the other five letters in the new series, eventually calling for words associated with each one and repeating over and over the name and sound of each letter.

"Excellent! Good job! And we can find so many words to connect with these letters, can't we? Our list can keep growing beyond the words we have just listed. We can even show how these letters may be in your child's name, right? We want to connect what we are learning to things that are meaningful to the children; to things that matter to the children; to things children know and care about – right? And, as we talk about these six letters with our children, then we want to ask them to match – to *match* – the letters. We match the letters with words, with pictures that use the letter. We match uppercase letters with lowercase letters. We *name*. We *point*. We *sound*. We *trace* and we *match*."

A spirited discussion ensues about uppercase and lowercase letters, almost entirely in Arabic, comparing concepts between the two languages. Nahed and the mothers go back and forth for more than two minutes. "I think you've got it, yes. I think you understand uppercase and lowercase," Nahed concludes, in English.

"Now I want to show you the materials you can use today," Nahed says, distributing more worksheets and plastic tubs containing crayons, magnetic letters and other supplies. "Remember that you do not have to use everything today. Follow what interests your child. You do not have to complete everything in class today. You are finding things that interest your child and that you can do when you get home. Today, maybe it is fun for your child to trace with a finger. Maybe they find that fun – for you and your child to trace with a finger. Maybe this morning, they only want to trace with a finger. That's OK. At home, you can trace with a crayon, with a pencil. Keep going. You want to keep it fun so they want to do more of this. It's OK to have fun while we learn. Fun is OK."

The parents are looking over the materials as Nahed suggests ideas for using each item. "As we do each week, we want you to use the first 20 minutes with the packet I am giving you, using the worksheets. There are many worksheets, so something should interest your child. They'll find something fun. So, 20 minutes for the packet, right?"

Heads nod. A few more brief questions shoot back and forth in Arabic.

"Yes, that's true," Nahed says, in English. "Maybe some children won't spend 20 minutes on the papers in this packet. And that's OK. Don't get frustrated. Try to do 20 minutes on the worksheets, but if your child won't do that – no problem. You can take these sheets home with you and do more of them when you have time at home. But please do try to spend, you know, about 20 minutes with the packet this morning. Then, that's the time – after 20 minutes – when we need to move to the hands-on activities. And what do I mean by *hands-on activities*?"

One mom holds up colorful magnetic letters from the tub. Another holds up a small, brightly illustrated board book (a small book with thick cardboard pages for each of the morning's six letters) from the tub.

"Yes, that works. Kids like magnet boards. Kids like the little books you've got there. They pick them up and use their hands to explore them. And remember that our magnet boards have both the uppercase letters and the lowercase letters, so you can do all kinds of things with those magnet boards. You can match uppercase and lowercase. You can ask for the sound of each letter. And we have flash cards, too, in your materials," she says, repeating the phrase, "Flash cards." Nahed pulls out six cards, all showing a letter from that morning's lesson, and fans them out to show off the colorful pictures. "Flash cards. Fun. Kids find fun things to do with flash cards."

"When we are done this morning, please ask me if you need extra sheets to take home – extra fun things to take home," Nahed continues. "Ask me at the end about this. And remember, we say: Don't try to do it all at once. Maybe focus on one letter each day, at home. Have fun with it."

The clock hits 9:45 and collectively, the mothers know it's time to move to the classroom where they will rejoin their children. Nahed calls out final instructions. "We go to the room with our children now. We are going now. There are water bottles and snack bars on the counter there. Take one if you didn't already. We are going now."

And in one lively procession, the mothers leave the first classroom.

In the Children's Classroom

"One goal in this session is to introduce the children to the material they will be learning with their moms, but we want everything in this session to be fun and very active," says Elizabeth Guglielmotti, talking about her children's classroom. During most of the week, she is an adult ESL instructor for ACCESS, but during the 10-week PCIL series, Elizabeth is the energetic leader of the 45-minute morning session with children while their parents are learning about the day's curriculum with Nahed down the hall. "We are giving the kids a head start on what their moms will be showing them later, but we also want this to be an experience of coming to school and leaving their moms and feeling safe and engaged in our activities. It helps that I already know many of the moms because they attend the ESL classes. I'm someone they know and trust. That makes this easier."

The mothers greet Elizabeth warmly at the doorway, and after several weeks in this series, only one mother needs to remain in the classroom to reassure her son. Elizabeth welcomes her, reassuring her that it's fine to stay one more week, and the mother comfortably settles in along the side of the class.

Elizabeth sits on the floor at one edge of several alphabet floor mats. The first activity of the morning gathers the children around her on the floor to watch a short alphabet video. The kids relax as the video plays. Afterward, Elizabeth invites them to recite portions of what they have just seen. They become more enthusiastic as she has them begin clapping along with the recitations.

Elizabeth Guglielmotti shows flash cards to the children.

She pulls out a stack of six new flash cards and begins going over them, one by one. The kids scoot across the floor to be closer to their teacher. Using call and response, she leads the children through naming "M," "N," "O," "P," "Q" and "R." With each letter, Elizabeth shows the card and names the picture on the card's opposite side.

Then it's time for some spirited singing. Elizabeth uses the alphabet song, set to the world's best-known tune for learning English letters. Also used by Mozart in the 1700s, the tune is known as, "Twinkle, Twinkle, Little Star" and "Baa, Baa, Black Sheep." Every American child seems to know the song, but, when the "ABC song" is first introduced in PCIL, it's new to some of the children who have recently arrived from exclusively Arabic-speaking communities. Nevertheless, just a few weeks into the PCIL series, some kids have already memorized the song sufficiently enough to sing along with their teacher and classmates.

Elizabeth understands the careful dance she needs to lead between high-energy, full-body activities and periods of calming games, so she pulls out the flash cards a second time. The kids form a tighter circle again, and she leads them through a second round of naming the six new letters.

Next, she shifts gears and returns to the high-energy games. Shepherding the kids to back away from one centrally placed alphabet floor mat, Elizabeth asks, "Who can find … 'A'?"

The kids look at each other, at Elizabeth and at the mat in the center of their circle.

"There's 'A!'" Elizabeth says, pointing. The children scramble to slap hands on the A, shown with a bright red apple. "'A' is for 'apple!'"

Now, the children are sprawled all over the alphabet mat, arms outstretched to touch the "A," so Elizabeth coaxes them back again to the edge of the mat. "Move away. Move away."

The kids move, but they also know what is coming next, so they eagerly watch Elizabeth's face until she calls for "B."

"'B!'" And they lunge at the B.

"'B' is for 'boat!'"

As she coaches them, they back up again.

Breanne Wainright helps Hasaina Wais learn to use scissors.

"'C!'" And, as the children scramble forward, "'C' is for 'clown!'"

Elizabeth continues all the way through "R."

The morning session in the children's room also includes a snack and more alphabet activities on the floor with Elizabeth. Before any girl or boy loses interest or expresses anxiety, it's suddenly 9:45 a.m. and time to reconnect with the mothers. Promptly, the parents come down the hallway from Nahed's classroom to claim their children and head into the interactive session.

Parent and Child Interactive Learning

Within seconds of stepping into the interactive classroom, the families are engaged. This room is twice the size of the room where the mothers first worked with Nahed, which is necessary to ensure plenty of room around the big, sturdy white tables where parents and children sit on black folding chairs and dig into the stacks of educational materials provided by Nahed and her team. Colorful posters and charts hung around the room reinforce the concepts the families are learning. After several weeks of PCIL sessions, the kids all know what is about to happen and they hurry to choose their chairs, climbing up beside their mothers to explore the provided resources. The mothers have learned to start with the worksheets in their packets and to place the more enticing objects in the big plastic tub just out of their child's immediate reach; they begin working with the six new letters. The official start time for this portion of the morning is 9:45, and within 60 seconds, more than half of the parents and children are noisily engaged.

The room's high ceiling and hard wooden floor soon echo with, "M! *Mmm*," and "N, *nnn*." The sounds begin almost in unison but soon overlap, as children move at different rates until the voices are a mixed chorus of chants, back and forth. The children's voices are often louder and clearer than their parents' tones.

Within three minutes, one mother has her son avidly focused on trying to make his fingertip trace the lines of a capital M on a worksheet. A line of upper- and lowercase M's fill the page in front of them and, one by one, the little boy conquers each shape. He is so intent on the activity that his finger rarely strays from the guidelines. After tracing, his mother offers him several crayons. He chooses a brown crayon and goes back over each "M" on the page, painstakingly trying to draw each one. His marks waiver a bit here and there, but this mother is having no problem engaging her son.

There are some questions in the room about these new letter shapes and the tiny arrows on the worksheets that indicate how to trace each shape. One mother waves at one of Nahed's aides – today it's Breanne Wainright from the ESL component of the program helping out in the classroom. Breanne stoops down as the mother asks about the proper strokes to form an "M." Breanne leans in between parent and child and slowly traces an "M." As she finishes, she says, "And we say, 'That's 'M,' *mmm*. Now you!"

The mother reaches out to repeat this action, but her son's finger beats her to the paper. He completes the motion. "And say it with me," Breanne says, "M, *mmm*." The boy does.

Now, the mother mimics the motion. Then, the boy repeats the motion again. They move across the page, through upper- and lowercase M's, tracing each one with their fingertips.

One little girl selects an orange crayon to trace the letters, picking up the crayon in her fist like a hand grasping a bar or a railing. She tries to trace the letter, but finds the crayon is positioned so awkwardly that it's difficult. Her mother gently opens her hand and forms her finger around the crayon in a more standard position for writing. The girl holds the crayon up in the air, flexing her fingers around it and observing her own hand. It's clearly a new feeling. Then, she goes back to tracing the letters – this time more successfully. As she finishes one worksheet, the girl reaches out for a different crayon, again using her fist to grasp it. Then, looking at her mother, the girl uses her own left hand to carefully place the crayon in a proper position in her right hand. Her mother nods and hugs her shoulder. The tracing continues.

> ### Tip for Success: Long-term Learning
> We continually reassure parents that the goal of our Interactive Learning sessions is not to have the children master everything introduced in these sessions. We present the Early Learning Content in small, manageable segments so that, even with limited English, the parents have a good opportunity to learn and practice the material with their children. The goal in the 10 PCIL sessions is not to master an entire early learning curriculum, but rather to show parents the importance of early learning in the home and to show them techniques and materials that they can continue to use there. As some children successfully master the content faster than others, it's easy to forget that the real goal is a long-term focus on learning in the home – both during and after the PCIL sessions. We repeat and reinforce this message in all of the 10 sessions.

Ten minutes into the 9:45 a.m. session, the first mother in the room has switched to using the hands-on activities in the plastic tub situated at the center of her table. The bright-red frame around the magnet board has caught her son's eye, so the mother positions the board in front of him on the table, picking out this week's letters from the bin and placing them randomly on the board for the boy to explore. His fingers carefully feel the letters, turning them around, and with some coaxing from his mother, he places them in the correct order along the top line of the magnet board.

Many of the parents already are adapting the resources and using them in ways Nahed did not even mention in her coaching session. One mother who is still using worksheets from the packet begins playing a game with the question, "Which way?" She takes one sheet at a time and lays it in front of her little girl, sometimes right side up and sometimes with the letters on the sheet upside down. "Which way?" she asks.

"This way," her daughter says softly, either pointing at a correctly placed paper or rotating an incorrectly placed paper 180 degrees, until the letters are properly oriented.

When her mother says, "Yes. Right," the little girl calls back, "Yay!"

Another parent lays out the six flash cards to the left of her child, then goes through the worksheets one by one, asking her son to name each letter and find that letter in the flash cards. He picks up each flash card and correctly matches it to the corresponding worksheet by proudly slapping it down onto the sheet with a crisp snap.

One boy spots the cans of Play-doh on a shelf at the back of the room. Nahed and her team haven't included Play-doh in the hands-on tubs this week, but this boy is drawn to the little row of canisters. Nahed is moving around the room, helping mothers if they request her assistance. The boy hops off his chair and points to the Play-doh.

"You want to use that?" Nahed asks. "*Play-doh*. You want to use Play-doh?"

He nods.

"What is it? *Play-doh*," Nahed coaches.

"Play-doh," he says.

"Yes, that's OK. What color do you want?"

The boy chooses red and reaches for it, but Nahed grabs it first and doesn't let him take the can. "You have to tell me: What color is this?"

He tilts his head as he looks from the can to her face.

"What color is this? It's red, isn't it? *Red*."

He frowns and pauses for a moment, but then says, loudly and clearly, "Red."

"Good," she says. "Go make something with the red Play-doh."

The boy begins flexing the modeling dough between his fingers, making a long string. But this whole exchange with Nahed has happened so quickly that his mother is surprised to find that he is working with Play-doh. She asks him about it in sharply enunciated Arabic.

"It's OK. *OK,*" Nahed tells her. "He asked me. He can use that to make letters. It's OK."

He pushes his red string into an arc, resembling the first hump in an "M."

Tip for Success: Let Your Child Lead

Children learn faster at a young age when they are able to attach their own meanings and interests to the material. That may involve focusing on each individual child's pre-ferred activities – while one enjoys coloring, another may want to use modeling dough. It also involves relating early concepts to things that matter to the young children. For example, if a child's favorite activity is soccer, it's easy to teach that a soccer ball is the shape of a circle. Or, when teaching letters, children often like to learn the letters that form their names.

By 10:15 a.m. in the interactive session, most children have tried coloring – usually reaching out to pick up crayons in a standard way from the start. But one more child, a small boy, now tries to grab a crayon in his fist and his mother has to coach him on the proper way to hold it. She must have shown him this earlier, because the moment she begins repositioning the crayon, he shakes his head and does this himself.

He knows. He just forgot. She smiles.

Nahed and her team spend the entire session silently observing, helping when asked and adding occasional words of encouragement. When one boy finishes an elaborate drawing with crayons, he spots Breanne and jumps off his chair to show her his sketch. She begins by praising it. "Beautiful," Breanne says, "That's great." Then, she adds, "Tell me the colors you've used."

The boy points to a brown circle but looks puzzled, remaining silent.

"Brown," Breanne says, and he repeats the word.

She points to another object on the page, and he identifies "Green."

They name one color after another. Breanne turns it into a kind of chant. If she says a word first, she adds, "Now you!" The boy picks up on this pattern and, even if he knows the color himself, he adds, "Now you!" They challenge each other. Some color combinations are beyond anyone's ability to identify. This game continues for nearly two minutes, until the boy returns to his mother and begins pointing at colors. The boy and his mother begin playing the same color-naming game together.

As Nahed moves around the room, she stops at one table and declares, "You are doing so well!" She is talking to the smallest girl in the room. The girl is sitting next to her mother, who exchanges a few words with Nahed in Arabic.

"Wow," Nahed says in English. "She's only 3 years old and she's been here only two months?" The mother nods, and Nahed continues, "So, to see her naming and sounding and tracing the letters like this! This is wonderful." The girl proudly grins and keeps coloring on her worksheets. She is one of the last kids in the entire classroom to stay with these worksheets, well after the 20-minute mark, as she finds lots of ways to use the sheets with her mother.

"She's picking this up so fast," Nahed says.

As the hands-on portion of this interactive session unfolds, the team finds that crayons are not the only physical challenges. Several of the children have pulled the plastic safety scissors from the tubs, as well as construction paper and glue sticks. One boy is a trendsetter – confidently cutting out letters and gluing them in rows on a dark green sheet of construction paper. Other children want to follow suit.

A girl sitting near him holds scissors in one fist and a sheet of blue paper in the other hand, moving them together in an awkward, uncertain way. Her mother looks perplexed and says something in Arabic. She gestures at her daughter's hands as if to place the scissors back into the tub.

"You want to use the scissors?" Breanne asks the girl, intervening at the table. The mother smiles up at her, welcoming the help. "Let me show you how to hold them," Breanne says.

She expertly forms the girl's hands and fingers around the scissors, and then holds the construction paper stiffly in front of the girl. Guiding the girl's hand to the crisp edge of the paper, Breanne shows her how to close her fingers together and make a neat slice with the scissors.

The girl's eyes pop at what she has done! Her mother nods in approval. Less than an inch away from the first slice, the girl attempts – and makes – another cut, all on her own. Breanne, who was holding the construction paper, now hands it to the girl, who is ready to hold both objects. Soon, the edge of the paper looks like the fringe around a rectangular rug.

The one boy who had his mother remain with him in the children's room at the start of the morning remains fairly quiet during this interactive session. He approaches each step of this session more thoughtfully than the other children. Silently, he explores each worksheet and then each object in the tub with his eyes and his fingers, flipping through the materials. He chooses the flash cards as his favorite for this session, examining each of the pictures and letters. He lays out the flash cards on the table and then finds each matching magnet letter in the tub to place atop each card. His mother brings out the board books. She begins to read the first book to him, but the boy shakes his head and places a hand on hers to close the cover. Instead, he wants to hold the stack of board books and sort them, matching each one with the corresponding flash card and magnet letter from his stack. Soon, he has six towers forming for each of the day's new letters, all properly matched and stacked from various alphabet objects he has found. His mother encourages and builds on this activity. She points at each letter stack, then names the letter – and, finally, he repeats each name. She sounds each letter – and he repeats. Eventually, he is talking with her using English names, sounds and words for the day's segment of the alphabet. Just a handful of English words pass between them, but they are clearly enunciated and properly used – and his pronunciation already is better than his mother's.

Tip for Success: Feedback Styles Vary

Through the years at ACCESS, we've learned a lot about the diversity of cultural expectations concerning our "feedback sessions." Many Americans assume it's always appropriate to honestly speak one's mind, but some cultures consider it disrespectful to criticize or even to question something that a respected teacher is doing. University of Michigan sociologist Dr. Wayne Baker has analyzed the relative values of self-expression around the world and finds that Americans rank among the most outspoken in the world. Many other cultures regard such public honesty as inappropriate and even insulting. If you are developing a program within an immigrant community, consider that you'll need to take great care in organizing the feedback process. In some cultures, it's a natural activity; in others it's a minefield. We find that feedback works best in relatively small groups; we strive for a positive tone in our exchanges; and we find that group feedback often is most effective in the form of informational questions and answers. If individuals have other issues to discuss or want to share pointed criticism, we meet with people more privately before or after class.

Parent Feedback Session

At 10:30 a.m., the parents crowd around one long table to talk with Nahed – mostly in Arabic, but also in occasional English. ACCESS to School is open to both men and women, from its ESL classes through its PCIL component, yet we have found that Yemeni-American women, in particular, are much more open to PCIL discussion and feedback if there are no men in the group. The dominance of women in our program matches demographic realities in Yemeni-American and Hispanic-American cultures, in which most of the men work on weekdays; in addition, most men have other opportunities outside the home to learn and practice English. This statistic also matches the cultural expectation that regards both childcare and early education as a mother's responsibility. At ACCESS, we remain open to participation by men, but we have observed that groups comprised of mothers surface the most robust discussions and feedback.

At 10:30 a.m., the children move to supervised but loosely structured childcare. Several of the children are intent on finishing work they began during the interactive session. A boy and a girl continue cutting and pasting letters, along with matching pictures, onto construction paper; other kids are playing with magnet boards or coloring. A couple of other children are enjoying snacks.

Nahed opens the feedback session with words of encouragement. "So good today! Very good!" Then, quickly invites questions. Hands and voices are raised all around the circle, so Nahed chooses who will go first. Because this session is so lively, she conducts most of it in Arabic, so that all of the mothers can understand the topics discussed. Throughout the session, however, Nahed regularly pauses to weave English into the conversation. The first topic the parents raise this morning concerns the widely varying preferences of their children.

After a couple of minutes of animated Arabic from several mothers, Nahed declares, "We always say: Don't push! Encourage!" She repeats, "Don't push! Instead we – " As her hands stretch out, calling for a response, the women answer, "Encourage."

One mother is not convinced and resumes the discussion. "My son won't do it! He won't sit!"

Nahed explains in English. "So, in this family, her son won't sit down to do the worksheets at home. He prefers hands-on activities. And that's OK. But take some of the extra worksheets with you, because you may find that your child will be interested in the future. You can go back and forth between activities. Encourage your child to do things that use the alphabet and numbers and all of the things we are learning. Play games. Have fun. So, maybe they won't touch a worksheet at home right now. They still can learn. And they may want to come back to the worksheets."

In mixed Arabic and English, the discussion turns to magnet boards. It's the single most popular hands-on activity in the classroom, several mothers agree. These rainbow-hued plastic sets are a whole new kind of activity for the children. Now the kids want magnet boards at home, but none of these mothers has one. One mother explains that crayons, markers, paper and most of the other supplies are available in many stores, but magnet boards are not.

"Around here: *Toys"R"Us*," says Nahed. "You know Toys"R"Us stores? They have magnet boards like these. And they're not too expensive." Extending the discussion in Arabic, the mothers discuss local shopping centers.

Then, a mother pulls out her smart phone and taps on it as she talks about "electronics" and complains about her child only wanting to "tap, tap, tap."

"That's OK," Nahed says. "If the electronics are popular, look for some of the good alphabet-learning games. There are a lot of good educational games for this age. I can help you find some good ones."

Another mother waves her hands dismissively and shrugs as she complains that she's got the opposite problem: no smart-phone and a child who only wants to color. Electronics aren't the answer in her home, she insists.

"That's OK, too," Nahed says. "We use what works. We want to follow our children's interests. We spend time with our children. We talk with our children. We listen to our children. We make time to have fun with letters and numbers and the things we are learning, right? We play games with our children. It's fun."

At this point, one mother brings up the growing popularity of scissors among the children, especially at the end of this morning's session. She shakes her head, saying that she's worried that her son might cut off a finger. She appeals to the other women and another parent voices a similar concern. One woman sighs.

Nahed responds in English, "No, of course you do not want to give your children sewing scissors or kitchen scissors. In class we only have the safety scissors. You can find these at the store.

Many stores have children's safety scissors. Safety scissors won't cut them."

The first mother holds up her hand like a stop sign and makes it clear that her child doesn't like the small, plastic or blunt-metal scissors. "They don't work! They don't cut!"

Nahed insists, "Yes, they will cut. They're not as sharp as your own scissors, but they will cut if you help your children learn how to hold the paper and the scissors."

Mothers start talking about their own experiences with scissors. Some laugh. Several women are talking at the same time.

"So, *anything else* we need to talk about?" Nahed asks raising her voice. The discussion is lively and shows no sign of waning, but she wants to close the scissors subject and make room for other feedback.

Finally, one mother explains in Arabic that she's worried about her son. "He doesn't want to come," she says. Even after several weeks, it's a struggle to convince the boy to get ready each Friday morning. Once they arrive, he's fine all morning long, she contends – but he's not happy about going to school with her every week.

"It takes time," Nahed says. "Don't worry. We all are working at this. And, when he does come with you, we will keep on showing him these fun activities – singing, dancing, the floor mats – and that he gets to spend time with you, too. He'll get in the habit."

The mother nods. Several other women chime in with words of encouragement. They've come a long way since starting the PCIL series, but they all still face challenges, the mothers say in Arabic and English.

At precisely 11 a.m., the morning session ends with a flurry of parents and children reuniting, pulling on their coats and heading toward the school's exit doors. By 11:05 a.m., Nahed and her team are left in the nearly empty classroom, reorganizing their tubs of supplies and straightening the furniture for another week.

Nahed Alkashbari with children in the Parent
and Child Interactive Learning group.

Our Resources

Amanda Morgan worked with Nahed Alkashbari in developing these lesson plans for the distinctive Parent and Child Interactive Learning component.

In building the program, we drew both on our significant experience with these components and the best practices used nationwide in English as a Second Language, parenting classes and case management. The resources we use in these three components – from lesson plans to worksheets and forms – are similar to those used in other programs. Some standard materials and resources are used in their entirety and combined with others to form a comprehensive curriculum, as is the case with ESL. In parenting education, we took a standard curriculum and modified it extensively to fit the needs of our population. For case management, we used best practices and strategies and created our own forms and procedures. But our greatest innovation was the creation of the Parent and Child Interactive Learning (PCIL) component for use with immigrant populations. So, for this resource section, we have chosen to show you detailed lesson plans for that one area of our much larger program.

As you look through these lesson plans, notice first that while the content and activities change throughout the weekly sessions, the structure of the sessions remains the same in the weeks that parents and children are in a particular phase of the program. Each lesson plan is structured around four key elements:

1. Raising parents' awareness of their children's development, learning and the importance of school readiness. In these lesson plans, you will see examples of the topics we raise with parents throughout the 10 weeks. You may choose to

use other examples as you raise the parents' awareness of developmental milestones appropriate for their children.

2. Teaching parents methods and strategies for engaging their children with the Early Learning Content both in our classroom and at home. Again, we show you the lesson plans, techniques and materials that are working for us. You may want to expand on our lists of materials.

3. Practicing techniques with parents that they, in turn, will use in ongoing interactions with their children. Building the parents' competence and confidence is really a crucial part of our program.

4. Partnering with parents as they move through the program by actively seeking their feedback and questions at the end of each session. If you organize this kind of program, you will be surprised at how actively parents will share fresh ideas, along with their concerns and questions.

Secondly, as you read these lesson plans, it's important to note that our Interactive Learning component is not intended to provide a comprehensive early childhood education in these 10 weekly, half-day sessions. We do not expect the children to master all of the material we are introducing by the end of the series. They certainly do learn many of the lessons we are teaching, but we have a larger and distinctively different goal in Interactive Learning: To teach parents about many kinds of educational materials and about the skills and strategies that they can use to successfully become the first teachers for their children. As we make parents aware of their children's developmental stages, we also introduce them to the array of learning materials they can bring into their homes – from safety scissors to alphabet magnet boards. In the Interactive Learning process, we show them how to interact with their children using specific materials and methods. The parents also learn teaching techniques that require no special materials – from identifying shapes and colors around the house to playing simple rhyming games. This builds their confidence as parents and helps them to perfect their skills. Over and over again, we see that these program elements produce parents who are empowered to take our 10-week training series as a starting point and make education and school preparation a major part of home life.

The following lesson plans are self-explanatory, with a little orientation:

Standard PCIL materials – Each lesson plan lists materials the teacher will need. The phrase "Standard PCIL Materials" includes resources that are common throughout the Interactive Learning sessions: a sign-in sheet for parents and children, a laptop computer, some kind of classroom projector with audio and video, pencils and crayons. We also have bottles of water and often a snack, such as a granola bar, available for the parents. This is part of our commitment to a safe learning community – a goal widely discussed among educators for improved learning in low-income and minority communities where a range of challenges may prevent full participation. In addition to ensuring physical and emotional safety in the program, this kind of learning environment considers all the needs of the participating parents and learners. Our goal is to create an environment that shows sincere support for our participants' well-being and academic success.

"Room A" and "Room B" – During each opening session, which we schedule from 9 to 9:45 a.m., parents and children are separated into different rooms (Room A and Room B) so that parents can learn and engage with the material before presenting it to their children. The main focus of this part of the session is teaching parents the information they need to know in order to be successful when they are brought back together with their children. This is key to working with immigrant parents, we have found – and is the piece that is missing in other mainstream school-readiness programs we have observed around the country. Our focus on preparing the parents before starting the parent-and-child portion of the day is key to our safe learning community, as it builds both confidence and expertise in parents, who are then able to share the day's lessons with their children. So, if you plan for such a program, be aware that you will need more than one room. (At the end of the morning session, we make use of Rooms A and B again, for our Feedback Time. Also note: Even though you will need a minimum of two rooms, we actually have three rooms available to us at Priest Elementary School, which gives our team even greater flexibility when organizing the weekly sessions.)

Schedule in Room A – In Room A, the teacher contributes to our safe learning community by first introducing parents to important awareness-raising topics. This part of the session is very important, as it helps the parents understand on a deeper level the changes they are seeing in their children's behavior, learning and development, as well as why school readiness is important (and what role they have in this). Next – depending on the English language ability of the parents – the teacher will review and teach new Early Learning Content. This includes reviewing material from earlier weeks and then teaching both the content (e.g., the target letters and their sounds) and the key words and directions the parents need to know (e.g., word "matching" in English). The teacher then moves to introducing and practicing these activities with the parents. Parents explore the materials, are introduced to fresh ideas for how to use these colorful resources and are taught strategies for each activity that will best engage their children. The teacher also discusses with parents how these activities can be modified for home use. Once the parents feel comfortable with the activities, the teacher facilitates a discussion in which parents can get clarification, ask questions and brainstorm how to handle potential challenges.

Schedule in Room B – Simultaneously, in Room B, a teacher is with the children, engaging them with songs and games and introducing the day's material in a fun and interesting way. Afterward, the children eat a healthy snack.

Back together in one classroom – We use the time from 9:45 to 10:30 a.m. to rejoin the children and parents. Now the parents become the teachers, using the materials and ideas they just explored in their own session. As their overall teacher for these 10 weeks, Nahed now steps back and lets the parents work with their children, while she remains in the room with other teaching aids to answer questions or offer reminders. For the first 20 minutes, parents are encouraged to work on the day's new lesson, encouraging their children to identify the new concepts and differentiate between the new content and what was covered in earlier sessions. After that, we encourage parents to move into hands-on activities that include manipulating objects and being creative with the provided materials. Often, children are so creative that they begin making their own connections or they wind up manipulating the resources in new ways. Parents are told that the number and depth of activities they complete during this portion of the morning will depend on the age, ability and interest of their children, and that they should let their children set the pace. The goal is not to complete a specific checklist of activities, but to spend as much time as possible following a child's own interest in exploring these new concepts. Working together with the support of the overall teacher, the parents are learning how to become successful educators in their own homes.

Feedback Time – From 10:30 to 11 a.m., parents and children separate again. While the children have a supervised playtime in Room B, the parents can focus without interruption on discussing what happened that morning in Room A. Feedback Time has two goals: To allow our professionals the opportunity to provide feedback to the whole group, and to give parents the chance to share their observations and questions. These sessions often surface a host of questions from parents. Parents are eager to raise practical issues, like where to buy glue sticks, as well as questions about the day's lesson, such as, "How can I tell if words really do rhyme?"

Lesson 1: Colors and Shapes

Materials:

- Standard PCIL materials
- Colors and Shapes songs/videos
- Colors and Shapes books
- Colors and Shapes flash cards
- Colors and Shapes floor mat

- Construction paper
- Scissors
- Glue
- Play-Doh
- Children's white board
- Shapes coloring pages
- Plastic or wooden blocks of various colors and shapes

Objectives:

Parents will be able to:
- Understand separation anxiety and strategies to use when facing it.
- Identify when to start teaching colors and shapes to their children.
- Determine age-appropriate Colors and Shapes activities for their children.
- Recognize easy activities for at-home practice.
- Practice with materials to build competency for working with their children later.

Children will be able to:
- Begin to identify colors: red, yellow, orange, pink, green, blue, purple, white, black, brown.
- Begin to identify shapes: circle, square, triangle, rectangle, oval, star.
- Begin to trace shapes.
- Begin to match shapes with objects.

Schedule: 9 to 9:45 a.m. At this time, parents and children gather in separate spaces, allowing parents to engage in the material before working with their children.

Parents (in Room A)

Tips for Awareness: The teacher goes over tips (like those listed below) as an exercise to encourage conversation and participation within the group. In efforts to build a safe learning community, the teacher also introduces parents to important awareness-raising topics. The teacher should open the discussion by asking parents to contribute their experiences or ideas, and then bring in the relevant information on these topics:

- Overcoming separation anxiety on the first day of school.
- Recognizing that separation anxiety is normal.
- Acknowledging why parents should not project their emotions onto their children when they leave, as being calm and positive will help children build coping skills.
- Bringing a familiar and comforting object to leave with a child.
- Establishing a routine for leaving. (For example, parents may put their children's things away, say goodbye and give a hug. Parents should not try not to sneak away. It may be easier for parents to do this in the beginning, but it is better for the attachment in the long run if children see their parents leave and learn to separate naturally.)
- Learning when children should be taught colors and shapes. (At 18 months, children should be taught colors; at 2 years, they should learn shapes.)
- Starting to learn colors and shapes by identifying things from the surrounding environment.
- Reassuring parents that the tips and guidelines discussed are general, and that they should not be worried if their children do not follow them precisely.

Introduction and/or review of Early Learning Content: The teacher will teach or review Early Learning Content with the parents, depending on their English language ability. Keep in mind that this may include teaching content, key words and important directions. Doing this will help parents complete the following Interactive Learning activities with their children with confidence:

- Identifying colors: red, yellow, orange, pink, green, blue, purple, white, black, brown.

- Recognizing shapes: circle, square, triangle, rectangle, oval, star.
- Teaching/reviewing key words (name, point, trace, match) and important directions.

Introduction and practice of PCIL activities: After reviewing the Early Learning Content, the teacher will introduce the Interactive Learning activities to parents step by step:

- Go over the Interactive Learning activities (see below for more details) that parents will be working on with their children.
- Have parents explore materials and practice activities. Elicit any other ideas parents may have for using the materials.
- Suggest strategies parents can use for each activity to get the most participation from their children.
- Ask parents to brainstorm how these activities may be modified for the home, and give examples.

Discussion, clarifications and questions: After parents feel comfortable with the Interactive Learning activities, the teacher will ask the parents if they have questions regarding the activities and how to implement them.

- Allow parents time to get clarification and ask questions about content, materials and activities.
- Facilitate discussion on what things may not go as planned with the children or what challenges parents may encounter. Then brainstorm what they can do to handle what comes up.

Children (in Room B)

Fun introduction to the material: The children's teacher should be introducing the children to the Early Learning Content in a fun and engaging way, which includes:

- Singing and dancing to songs about shapes and colors.

- Using games to practice identifying target shapes and colors.
- Identifying shapes and colors throughout the room (and perhaps even using a floor mat with colors and shapes).

After the fun introduction, children should sit down together and have a healthy snack before rejoining their parents.

Schedule: 9:45 to 10:30 a.m. At this time, parents and children come together in one classroom. Parents are provided with all materials for all of the activities, but it is up to each parent to decide which activities his/her child should complete. The pace at which parents and children move through the activities is dependent on the child's ability, interest and engagement in each activity. For the first 20 minutes, we indicate that parents should focus on practicing the Early Learning Content (activities 1-3 below) with their children. For the remaining time, parents should move on to hands-on activities (activities 4-6 below) with their children. Whatever the participants do not get through, we recommend that they try at home. Throughout the activities, teachers float around the room, helping with activities as needed and providing individual coaching and feedback for the parents.

Parent and Child Interactive Learning activities:

1. Name colors and shapes.
- Parents show a shape/color to their children on a worksheet.
- Parents ask their children, "What shape/color is this?" Children should respond with the appropriate shape or color. Our parents are coached to start by asking for basic shapes, such as a square, triangle or circle.
- If a child does not recognize a shape/color, the parent says the name of the shape/color to the child, who repeats it.
2. Point to colors and shapes.
- Parents name the shape/color that they want their children to point to. For example, "Point to the circle."

- If a child is not able to find a shape/color, the parent should help him/her find and point to the correct shape/color, and say, "This is the circle."

3. Trace shapes.
- Using a worksheet, children should identify a shape on the paper and then trace it with a finger.

4. Find colors and draw shapes.
- For this activity, parents have their children practice both colors and shapes together. Parents are provided with boxes of crayons containing the target colors.
- Parents choose a crayon color (e.g., "Get a green crayon.") and then tell their children to draw a specific shape with that crayon (e.g., "Now draw a square.").

5. Match shapes and colors with objects in the room.
- Parents point to a color/shape on their children's desk, asking them to identify an object in their surroundings that is the same color/shape.

6. Use hands-on materials for interactive play.
- Play-Doh: Children can form shapes out of Play-Doh.
- Books and magazines: Parents ask their children to point out, name and find colors and shapes within a book or magazine. Depending on the material provided, children may be able to cut out images of certain colors or shapes and glue them to another piece of paper.
- Flash cards: Parents can practice colors and shapes by showing children a flash card and asking for the name of the color or shape on the card; alternatively, children may want to match colors and shapes from the cards to items in the room. Parents also may give multiple cards to their children and ask them to select a particular color or shape.
- Plastic or wooden blocks: Parents can ask their children to place blocks that are the same color or shape together; parents can also say a color or shape and then ask their children to hold up the correct block. In addition, children can trace blocks using crayons or a pencil on a piece of

paper and then practice identifying the shapes from the paper instead of from the blocks.

Schedule: 10:30 to 11 a.m. At this time, parents and children separate again. Parents and teachers exchange feedback while the children enjoy structured playtime. The children may also continue engaging in the hands-on activities provided earlier in the lesson. Some children may want to complete projects they started during their time with parents.

Parents (in Room A)

Feedback (from parents):
- What worked well?
- What did not work well?
- What might have made the activities more successful?
- Did any of the concerns or potential challenges you mentioned earlier come up? If so, how did you handle them?
- What do you think you can do at home to continue to help your child learn?

Feedback (to parents):
- Give lots of encouragement.
- Note the general observations of the facilitator.
- Generate additional ideas the parents can take home to continue the learning process.

Children (in Room B)

Structured playtime with games, activities and videos.

Lesson 2: Letter Recognition – Aa, Bb, Cc, Dd, Ee, Ff

- Standard PCIL materials
- Alphabet songs/videos
- Alphabet books
- Alphabet flashcards with pictures
- Magnet board
- Alphabet mat
- Construction paper
- Scissors
- Glue
- Magnet letters: Aa, Bb, Cc, Dd, Ee, Ff
- Children's white board
- Coloring worksheets with pictures of things that start with the target letter
- Uppercase and lowercase matching worksheets
- Magazines and newspapers

Objectives:

Parents will be able to:
- Understand the basics of how to begin teaching letters to their children.
- Determine age-appropriate letter recognition activities for their children.
- Recognize easy activities for at-home practice.
- Practice with materials to encourage child learning.

Children will be able to:
- Begin naming the letters: Aa, Bb, Cc, Dd, Ee, Ff.
- Begin making the sounds of the letters: Aa, Bb, Cc, Dd, Ee, Ff.

- Begin tracing the letters: Aa, Bb, Cc, Dd, Ee, Ff.
- Begin matching target letters with appropriate pictures.
- Begin matching uppercase and lowercase letters.

Schedule: 9 to 9:45 a.m. Parents and children gather in separate spaces.

Parents (in Room A)

Tips for Awareness: The teacher goes over tips (like those listed below) as an exercise to encourage conversation and participation within the group – thereby helping to build a safe learning community and introducing parents to important awareness-raising topics. The teacher should open the discussion by asking parents to contribute their experiences or ideas, and then bring in the relevant information on these topics:

- Q: Which is taught first – letters or letter sounds?
- A: Letters are taught first. Letters give clues for sound and labels; letter sounds are too abstract, and aren't consistent enough for young children.
- Q: Which is taught first – uppercase letters or lowercase letters?
- A: We start with uppercase letters when working with young children.

Introduction and/or review of Early Learning Content:

- Teach/review name and sound of letters: Aa, Bb, Cc, Dd, Ee, Ff.
- Teach/review the key words (name, point, sound, trace, find, match) and important directions.

Introduction and practice of PCIL activities (see Lesson 1)

Discussion, clarifications and questions (see Lesson 1)

Children (in Room B)

A fun introduction to the material: The children's teacher should be introducing the children to the Early Learning Content in a fun and engaging way, including:

- Singing and dancing to alphabet songs.
- Using games to practice naming target letters.
- Identifying target letters throughout the room (perhaps even using an alphabet floor mat or other helpful and colorful objects).

After the fun introduction, the children should sit down together and have a healthy snack before meeting up with their parents.

Schedule: 9:45 to 10:30 a.m. At this time, parents and children come together in one classroom. Parents are provided with all materials for all of the activities, but it is up to each parent to decide which activities their child should complete. The pace at which parents and children move through the activities is dependent upon a child's abilities, interest and engagement in each activity. For the first 20 minutes, we indicate that parents should focus on practicing the Early Learning Content (activities 1-6 below) with their children. For the remaining time, parents should move on to hands-on activities (activities 7-9 below) with their children. Whatever the participants do not get through, we recommend that they try at home. Throughout the activities, teachers float around the room, helping with activities as needed and providing individual coaching and feedback for the parents.

Parent and Child Interactive Learning activities:

1. Name letters.
- Parents show letters to their children on a worksheet.
- Parents ask their children, "What letter is this?" Children should respond with the appropriate answer.
- If a child does not recognize a letter, the parent says the name of the letter to the child, who repeats it.
- Advanced option: Parents ask their children to say the name of a word that begins with each letter, e.g., "A – apple," "B – banana," "C – cat."
2. Point to letters.
- Parents name the letters that they want their children to point to. For example, "Point to the letter A."

- If a child is not able to find a letter, the parent should help him/her find and point to the correct letter, and then say, "This is A."

3. Sound out letters.
- Parents name a letter and then immediately say the sound of the letter to their children. Parents ask their children to point to the letter and repeat the letter name and sound.
- Advanced option: Parents have many letters in front of their child. Parents ask, "What letter makes this sound…?" The child points to the letter that makes that sound and then repeats the sound to the parent.

4. Trace letters.
- Using a worksheet, parents have their children first identify a letter on a piece of paper and then trace it with a finger.
- Once the child has traced the letter with a finger, parents give instructions on how to properly hold a pencil. Using the pencil, the child can now trace the letter again.

5. Match letters with pictures.
- Parents use worksheets to show their children pictures of animals, places, objects and toys (along with their corresponding letters).
- Parents ask their children to point to a picture that starts with a particular letter. The parent should also make the sound of the letter. The child should then complete the worksheet by matching the letter with the correct picture. (A parent can assist with this if needed.)
- Advanced option: Put letter and picture flashcards together and mix them up. Parents can ask their children to match each letter with the picture that starts with that letter.

6. Match uppercase with lowercase.
- Parents create a worksheet by writing uppercase letters on one side of a piece of paper and lowercase letters on the opposite side.
- Parents give their children a crayon or pencil and ask them to draw a line connecting the two letters that are the same.

▪ Advanced option: The parent can ask the child to say the sound of the letter while they are drawing the line.

7. Find letters.

▪ Parents give their children multiple letters to choose from on a worksheet, on flashcards or on magnets, and say, "Can you find the letter A?"

▪ If the child is not able to find the letter, the parent should help him/her find the correct letter and say, "This is A."

▪ Advanced option: The parent writes down a small word such as "apple" or "dog" for the child and then asks where a letter is within that word. When the child finds the letter, the parent repeats the letter and then says the entire word, dragging his/her finger across the letters and sounding them out slowly.

8. Color letters.

▪ Parents provide their children with crayons and construction paper. Parents ask their children to color a letter with a specific color, using the crayons.

▪ Advanced option: After the child is done coloring, ask him/her to name the letter, sound, color and then also a word that starts with that letter.

9. Utilize hands-on materials for interactive play.

▪ Play-Doh: Children can form letters out of Play-Doh.

▪ Books and magazines: Parents ask their children to point out, name and find letters in a book or magazine. Depending on the material provided, children may be able to cut out letters and glue them to another piece of paper.

▪ Flash cards: Parents can practice letters by showing children a flash card and asking for the name of the letter on the card; parents may also give multiple cards to their children and ask them to select a particular letter.

▪ Magnet board or cookie sheet with magnet letters: Children can name, sort, sound and match letters using a board. Some children may also be able to spell words, such as their name, on the board.

Schedule: 10:30 to 11 a.m. At this time, parents and children separate again. Parents and teachers exchange feedback in Room A while the children are enjoying structured playtime in Room B. (See Lesson 1 for more details.)

Lesson 3: Letter Recognition – Gg, Hh, Ii, Jj, Kk, Ll

Materials:

- Standard PCIL materials
- Alphabet materials listed in Lesson 2
- Magnet letters: Gg, Hh, Ii, Jj, Kk, Ll

Objectives:

Parents will be able to:
- Complete the same objectives listed in Lesson 2 except with this week's new letters.

Children will be able to:
- Complete the same objectives listed in Lesson 2 except with this week's new letters.

Schedule: 9 to 9:45 a.m. Again, parents and children gather in separate spaces.

Parents (in Room A)

Tips for Awareness: The teacher goes over tips (like those listed below) as an exercise to encourage conversation and participation within the group, helping to build a safe learning community and also to introduce parents to these important awareness-raising topics. The teacher should open the discussion by asking parents to contribute their experiences or ideas, and then bring in the relevant information on these topics:

- What it means to be "ready for school" in the U.S. In the early weeks of our series of 10 sessions, we talk to parents about cultural differences in expectations concerning the education of infants and children through age 4. We explain that, in America, parents are expected to begin introducing basic concepts such as letters, numbers, shapes and so on to prepare their children for school.
- Physical well-being and motor development (gross and fine-motor skills).
- Social and emotional development – the ability to interact with others and control/express emotions appropriately.
- Approaches to learning – using enthusiasm, curiosity and persistence for tasks.
- Language development – communication skills and emergent literacy.
- Cognition and general knowledge – thinking and problem-solving, as well as a general understanding of the way the world works.

Introduction and/or review of Early Learning Content:
- Review name and sound of letters from last week; introduce this week's new letters.
- Teach/review the key words (name, point, sound, trace, find, match) and important directions.

Introduction to and practice of PCIL activities (see Lesson 1)
Discussion, clarifications and questions (see Lesson 1)

Children (in Room B)

Fun introduction to the material (see Lesson 2)

Schedule: 9:45 to 10:30 a.m. At this time, parents and children come together in one classroom. Parents are provided with all materials for all of the activities, but it is up to each parent to decide which activities their child should complete. (See Lesson 2.)

- (See Lesson 2 for letter-related activities 1-9.)

Schedule: 10:30 to 11 a.m. At this time, parents and children separate again. In Room A, parents and teachers exchange feedback while the children are enjoying structured playtime in Room B. (See Lesson 1 for more details.)

Lesson 4: Letter Recognition – Mm, Nn, Oo, Pp, Qq, Rr

Materials:

- Standard PCIL materials
- Alphabet materials listed in Lesson 2
- Magnet Letters: Mm, Nn, Oo, Pp, Qq, Rr

Objectives:

Parents will be able to:
- Complete the same objectives listed in Lesson 2 except with this week's new letters.

Children will be able to:
- Complete the same objectives listed in Lesson 2 except with this week's new letters.

Schedule: 9 to 9:45 a.m. Again, parents and children gather in separate spaces.

Parents (in Room A)

Tips for Awareness: The teacher goes over tips (like those listed below) as an exercise to encourage conversation and participation within the group, helping to build a safe learning community and also to introduce parents to these important awareness-raising topics. The teacher should open the discussion by asking parents to contribute their experiences or ideas, and then bring in the relevant information on these topics:

- Cognitive/developmental milestones for 3-year-olds that include learning by doing, absorbing information through the senses, reciting cause/effect relationships and matching pictures to objects.
- Cognitive/developmental milestones for 3-year-olds that include learning by doing and learning through the senses, understanding the difference between fantasy and reality, starting to develop logical thinking and recognizing patterns.

Introduction and/or review of Early Learning Content:

- Review the names and sounds of letters from earlier sessions; introduce this week's new letters.
- Teach/review the key words (name, point, sound, trace, find, match) and important directions.

Introduction to and practice of PCIL activities (see Lesson 1)
Discussion, clarifications and questions (see Lesson 1)

Children (in Room B)

Fun introduction to the material (see Lesson 2)

Schedule: 9:45 to 10:30 a.m. At this time, parents and children come together in one classroom. Parents are provided with all materials for all of the activities, but it is up to each parent to decide which activities their child should complete. (See Lesson 2.)

Parent and Child Interactive Learning activities:

- (See Lesson 2 for letter-related activities 1-9.)

Schedule: 10:30 to 11 a.m. At this time, parents and children separate again. In Room A, parents and teachers exchange feedback while the children are enjoying structured playtime in Room B. (See Lesson 1 for more details.)

Lesson 5: Letter Recognition – Ss, Tt, Uu, Vv, Ww, Xx, Yy, Zz

Materials:

- Standard PCIL materials
- Alphabet materials listed in Lesson 2
- Magnet letters: Ss, Tt, Uu, Vv, Ww, Xx, Yy, Zz

Objectives:

Parents will be able to:

- Complete the same objectives listed in Lesson 2 except with this week's new letters.

Children will be able to:

- Complete the same objectives listed in Lesson 2 except with this week's new letters.

Schedule: 9 to 9:45 a.m. Again, parents and children gather in separate spaces.

Parents (in Room A)

Tips for Awareness: The teacher goes over tips like those listed below as an exercise to encourage conversation and participation within the group, helping to build a safe learning community and also introducing parents to these important awareness-raising topics. The teacher should open the discussion by asking parents to contribute their experiences or ideas, and then bring in the relevant information on these topics:

- Language milestones for 3-year-olds that include having 75 percent of speech be understandable, using complete sentences of three to five words and starting to understand and use the words "now, soon, later," etc.
- Language milestones for 3-year-olds that include possessing a 1,500-word vocabulary, understanding how

words relate to one another, starting to understand and use the words "if, why, when," etc.

Introduction and/or review of Early Learning Content:

- Review name and sound of letters from earlier sessions; introduce this week's new letters.
- Teach/review the key words (name, point, sound, trace, find, match) and important directions.

Introduction to and practice of PCIL activities (see Lesson 1)
Discussion, clarifications and questions: (see Lesson 1)

Children (in Room B)

Fun introduction to the material (see Lesson 2)

Schedule: 9:45 to 10:30 a.m. At this time, parents and children come together in one classroom. Parents are provided with all materials for all of the activities, but it is up to each parent to decide which activities their child should complete. (See Lesson 2)

Parent and Child Interactive Learning activities:

- (See Lesson 2 for letter-related activities 1-9.)

Schedule: 10:30 to 11 a.m. At this time, parents and children separate again. In Room A, parents and teachers exchange feedback while the children are enjoying structured playtime in Room B. (See Lesson 1 for more details.)

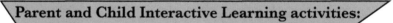

Lesson 6: Alphabet Book

Materials:

- Standard PCIL materials
- Alphabet materials listed in Lesson 2
- Magnet letters of the entire alphabet

Objectives:

Parents will be able to:

- Identify strategies for learning and reviewing the alphabet with their child.
- Understand how to create a book using their children's knowledge of the alphabet.
- Recognize easy ways to make an alphabet book using materials from home.
- Practice with materials to encourage child-learning.

Children will be able to:

- Continue learning to name the letters of the alphabet.
- Continue learning to sound out the letters of the alphabet.
- Continue learning to match letters with pictures.
- Begin creating an alphabet book (with a parent's help).

Schedule: 9 to 9:45 a.m. Again, parents and children gather in separate spaces.

Parents (in Room A)

Tips for Awareness: The teacher goes over tips (like those listed below) as an exercise to encourage conversation and participation within the group, helping to build a safe learning community and to introduce parents to these important awareness-raising topics. The teacher should open the discussion by asking parents to contribute their experiences or ideas, and then bring in the relevant information on these topics:

Strategies for learning the alphabet with your child. These include:

- Connecting letters to things that are meaningful to the child whenever possible. For example, focus on letters that are in the child's name.
- Focusing on one letter per day/week.
- Writing everywhere, including the playground, bathtub, grocery store and other fun places.
- Pointing out letters/numbers in your environment.

- Reading books together.
- Filling your home with words and letters.

Introduction and/or review of Early Learning Content:

- Review letters and lessons – name, sound, point, trace and match all letters of the alphabet.

Introduction and practice of PCIL activities: After reviewing the Early Learning Content, the teacher will introduce the Interactive Learning activities to parents step by step:

- The teacher displays example books, explains the guidelines for the project, and provides materials that the parent-and-child team may utilize during their book's creation.
- The teacher models how to create a page of the book using materials provided.
- Parents are asked to explore materials and practice activities they may use during the creation of the book. We elicit any other ideas parents may have for using materials in the book.
- Parents plan their own book before meeting with their children.
- Parents are asked to brainstorm other activities that may be useful when working on the book at home, particularly because they will not complete this project in class.

Discussion, clarifications and questions (see Lesson 1)

Children (in Room B)

Fun introduction to the material (see Lesson 2)

Schedule: 9:45 to 10:30 a.m. At this time, parents and children come together in one classroom.

For the first 10-20 minutes, parents should focus on reviewing the alphabet with their children using the Interactive Learning activities found in Lesson 2. Parents and children can complete any of activities 1-6, focusing on letters and sounds that are challenging for the child. After children are able to complete these activities with confidence, they may move on to creating their alphabet book.

Throughout the activities, teachers should be floating around the room, helping with the book creation as needed and providing individual coaching and feedback for the parents. At the beginning of the session, parents are provided with all the materials for the activities below, but it is up to the each parent to decide which activities their child should complete. Some parent-and-child teams may focus on the Early Learning Content, while others may start creating their alphabet book right away. The pace at which the parent and child move is dependent on the child's interests, abilities and engagement in each activity.

Parent and Child Interactive Learning activities:

1. Review the alphabet.
- (See Lesson 2 for the list of activities 1-6.)
2. Follow alphabet book guidelines.
- Ensure that each page contains one letter (upper- and lowercase) and at least one picture.
- Note that choosing pictures for each letter may be the most fun for the child. The parents should allow their children to find as many pictures as they would like to reinforce the letter.
- Allow children to use construction paper, markers, glue, crayons and other materials to create their book.
- Have parents ask their children to find the letters for their book in newspapers or magazines.
- Confirm that children are identifying the letters, cutting, gluing and coloring the pages with parental guidance.
- Make parents aware that they should use this book as a review exercise for their children when it is completed.

Schedule: 10:30 to 11a.m. At this time, parents and children separate again. In Room A, parents and teachers exchange feedback while the children are enjoying structured playtime in Room B. (See Lesson 1 for more details.)

Lesson 7: Counting Numbers 1-10

Materials:

- Standard PCIL materials
- Number songs/videos
- Number books
- Number flashcards with pictures
- Magnet board
- Number mat
- Construction paper
- Scissors
- Glue
- Magnet numbers: 0-9
- Children's white board
- Popsicle sticks

Objectives:

Parents will be able to:

- Identify what counting skills their children need to have before entering school.
- Determine age-appropriate counting activities for their children.
- Recognize easy activities for at-home practice.
- Practice with materials to encourage child learning.

Children will be able to:

- Begin naming numbers one through 10.
- Begin tracing numbers one through 10.
- Begin counting with numbers one through 10.
- Begin matching numbers one through 10 with pictures.

Schedule: 9 to 9:45 a.m. Again, parents and children gather in separate spaces.

Tips for Awareness: The teacher goes over tips (like those listed below) as an exercise to encourage conversation and participation within the group, helping to build a safe learning community and to introduce parents to these important awareness-raising topics. The teacher should open the discussion by asking parents to contribute their experiences or ideas, and then bring in the relevant information on these topics:

Understanding numbers and counting skills before school:
- Children should be curious about numbers/counting before starting school.
- Children should be able to count five objects as well as to put the numbers one to five in order.
- Children should understand the concepts of quantity and should recognize words such as "more," "less," etc.

Introduction and/or review of Early Learning Content:

- Teach/review numbers one through ten.
- Teach/review the key words (name, point, sound, trace, find, match, count) and important directions.

Introduction and practice of PCIL activities (see Lesson 1)
Discussion, clarifications and questions (see Lesson 1)

Children (in Room B)

Fun introduction to the material: The children's teacher should be introducing the children to the Early Learning Content in a fun and engaging way, including:

- Singing and dancing to number songs.
- Using games to practice numbers.
- Identifying target numbers throughout the room (perhaps even using a numbered floor mat or other helpful and colorful objects).

After the fun introduction, the children should sit down together and have a healthy snack before meeting up with their parents.

Schedule: 9:45 to 10:30 a.m. At this time, parents and children come together in one classroom. Parents are provided with all materials for all of the activities, but it is up to each parent to decide which activities their child should complete. The pace at which parents and children move through the activities is dependent upon the child's abilities, interest and engagement in each activity. For the first 20 minutes, we indicate that parents should focus on practicing the Early Learning Content (activities 1-3 below) with their children. For the remaining time, parents should move on to hands-on activities (activities 4-5 below) with their children. Whatever the participants do not get through, we recommend that they try at home. Throughout the activities, teachers float around room, helping with activities as needed and providing individual coaching and feedback for the parents.

Parent and Child Interactive Learning activities:

1. Name numbers.
   - Parents shows numbers to their children on a worksheet.
   - Parents asks their children, "What number is this?" Children should respond with the appropriate answer.
   - If the child does not recognize the number, the parent says the name of the number to the child, who repeats it.
2. Point to numbers.
   - Parents name the numbers that they want their children to point to. For example, "Point to number two."
   - If a child is not able to find the number, the parent should help the child find and point to the correct number and say, "This is two."
3. Color numbers.
   - Parents provide their children with crayons and a worksheet of multiple objects, such as 10 apples, five dogs or three cats.
   - Parents will ask their children to color a certain number of objects.
4. Match numbers with pictures.

- Parents use flashcards, videos and books to show pictures of animals, places and toys in different quantities.
- Parents name a number and asks their children to point to the picture that contains the correct number of objects.

5. Count.

- Parent asks the child to count objects around the room, a person's fingers and any other elements in the surroundings that interest the child. Parent should count with the child.
- Parents also can ask children to jump, stomp or clap for a certain number of times. Parents should count with the children.
- Play "Pick Up Sticks" with children by designating a certain number of sticks to be picked up during each turn.

Schedule: 10:30 to 11 a.m. At this time, parents and children separate again. In Room A, parents and teachers exchange feedback while the children are enjoying structured playtime in Room B. (See Lesson 1 for more details.)

Lesson 8: Size and Comparison

Materials:

- Standard PCIL materials
- Size and Comparison songs/videos
- Size and Comparison books
- Size and Comparison flashcards with pictures
- Magnet board
- Colored blocks of various shapes
- Construction paper
- Scissors
- Glue

■ Children's white board

Parents will be able to:
■ Understand the basic concepts of size and comparison that their children will need to know as they prepare for school.
■ Identify simple ways to teach children concepts of size and comparison in this lesson ("same and different," "short and long," "big and small").
■ Determine age-appropriate Size and Comparison activities for their child.
■ Recognize easy activities for at-home practice.
■ Practice with materials to encourage child learning.

Children will be able to:
■ Begin identifying "same and different," "short and long," "big and small."
■ Begin circling "same and different," "short and long," "big and small."
■ Begin to copy, cut, glue and color "same and different," "short and long," "big and small."

Schedule: 9 to 9:45 a.m. Again, parents and children gather in separate spaces.

Parents (in Room A)

Tips for Awareness: The teacher goes over tips (like those listed below) as an exercise to encourage conversation and participation within the group, helping to build a safe learning community and introducing parents to these important awareness-raising topics. The teacher should open the discussion by asking parents to contribute their experiences or ideas, and then bring in the relevant information on these topics:

Understanding basic concepts of comparison and size:

- Before starting school, children will need to learn the basic concepts of comparison and sizes, which include location, amount, description, time, intensity and feelings.
- Use real and tangible objects when teaching a child. For example, when teaching "on and off," turn the lights in the house on and off.
- Practice reading as another great way to teach children these concepts.
- While just a few sizes and comparisons are learned in the classroom – "same and different," "short and long," "big and small" – parents should look for other sizes and comparisons to teach children at home and in their neighborhood.

Introduction and/or review of Early Learning Content:

- Teach/review the key words "same and different," "short and long," "big and small."
- Ensure parents understand each concept and how to differentiate each one.

Introduction and practice of PCIL activities (see Lesson 1)
Discussion, clarifications and questions (see Lesson 1)

Children (in Room B)

Fun introduction to the material: The children's teacher should be introducing the children to the Early Learning Content in a fun and engaging way, including:

- Singing and dancing to relevant songs.
- Using games to practice identifying sizes and comparisons.
- Identifying sizes and comparing objects throughout the room (perhaps even using a related floor mat or other helpful and colorful objects).

After the fun introduction, the children should sit down together and have a healthy snack before meeting up with their parents.

Schedule: 9:45 to 10:30 a.m. At this time, parents and children come together in one classroom. For the first 20 minutes, we indicate that parents should focus on practicing the Early Learning Content (activities 1-3 below) with their children. For the remaining time, parents should move on to hands-on activities (activity 4 below) with their children. Whatever the participants do not get through, we recommend that they try at home.

Parent and Child Interactive Learning activities:

1. Identify sizes and comparisons.
   - Using objects of a variety of sizes and shapes, parents ask children about comparisons between two objects. For example, holding up two different size blocks, parents might ask, "Which one is big?" Or, holding up two different size pencils, parents might ask, "Which one is short?"
   - Using a worksheet, parents point to pictures and ask their children about the differences.
   - Parents also ask children to match things that are the same.
2. Circle "big," "small," "short," etc.
   - Using a worksheet or real objects, parents ask children to circle (with a pencil or finger) the object that is the big, small, short or long one, selecting from a group of objects provided.
3. Find sizes and comparisons.
   - Using magazines and newspapers, parents help children cut out objects from pictures that are short, long, small, big, different and the same.
   - Parents ask children to place the pictures in categories.
   - Parents ask why certain pictures were chosen, why these pictures were placed in a particular category, and encourage children to think about comparing them with other objects around the room.
4. Use hands-on materials for interactive play.

- Play-Doh: Children can form objects out of Play-Doh and then compare the objects they have made with the new words: "big" and "small," etc.
- Flash cards: Parents invite children to practice sizes and comparisons by showing children two flash cards with objects on them and asking for objects that are "big" and "small," etc.
- Plastic or wooden blocks: Children can sort blocks of the same shape or size or parents can hold up blocks of different sizes and shapes and ask for a comparison.

Schedule: 10:30 to 11 a.m. At this time, parents and children separate again. In Room A, parents and teachers exchange feedback while the children are enjoying structured playtime in Room B. (See Lesson 1 for more details.)

Lesson 9: Rhyming

Materials:

- Standard PCIL materials
- Nursery rhyme songs/videos
- Rhyming books
- Construction paper
- Scissors
- Glue
- Children's white board

Objectives:

Parents will be able to:
- Build their own phonological awareness.
- Determine age-appropriate rhyming activities for their children.

- Recognize easy activities for at-home practice.
- Practice with materials to encourage child learning.

Children will be able to:
- Begin to understand what "rhyming" means.
- Begin to identify rhyming words.
- Begin to match rhyming words.
- Begin singing along to songs that rhyme.

Schedule: 9 to 9:45 a.m. Again, parents and children gather in separate spaces.

Parents (in Room A)

Tips for Awareness: The teacher goes over tips (like those listed below) as an exercise to encourage conversation and participation within the group, helping to build a safe learning community and introducing parents to these important awareness-raising topics. The teacher should open the discussion by asking parents to contribute their experiences or ideas, and then bring in the relevant information on these topics:

Understanding phonological awareness, or the ability to hear the sound structure of a word or parts of words. This helps children to:
- Match word endings.
- Match word beginning sounds.
- Find collections of familiar sounds.
- Rearrange word sounds to make up new words.
- Apply these concepts when learning to read.

Introduction and/or review of Early Learning Content:
- Teach/review the basic concepts and mechanics of rhyming.
- Go over examples and learn some common rhyming sounds.

Introduction and practice of PCIL activities (see Lesson 1)
Discussion, clarifications and questions (see Lesson 1)

Children (in Room B)

Fun introduction to the material: The children's teacher should be introducing the children to the Early Learning Content in a fun and engaging way, including:

- Singing and dancing to nursery rhymes.
- Using games to identify rhyming words.
- Identifying things throughout the room that rhyme. We have seen children turn this activity into a game that they enjoy playing at home.

After the fun introduction, the children should sit down together and have a healthy snack before meeting up with their parents.

Schedule: 9:45 to 10:30 a.m. At this time, parents and children come together in one classroom. For the first 20 minutes, we indicate that parents should focus on practicing the Early Learning Content (activity 1 below) with their children. For the remaining time, parents should move on to hands-on activities (activities 2-3 below) with their children. Whatever the participants do not get through, we recommend that they try at home.

Parent and Child Interactive Learning activities:

1. Identify rhyming words.
- Worksheets are provided with rhyming words and related pictures.
- For children who can't read, parents show pictures of two objects that rhyme on the sheets. Parents ask, "What is this?" Children respond with the name of each object. Parents go back and forth, sounding the name, then ask, "Do they sound the same?" Parents encourage children to hear sounds that are the same within the words. "They rhyme because they sound the same."

2. Match rhyming words with objects.
- Parents present two or three sets of rhyming words using pictures of objects.

- Parents ask children to name the objects, then ask which ones sound the same. If this is too difficult for children, parents point to the objects and say the words, repeating the process until the children try to guess.

3. Sing nursery rhymes.
- Many nursery rhymes and songs with easy-to-hear rhymes are available online or in books. Practice these songs with children in rhythm. As we sing, we place a heavier emphasis on the rhyming words within the song.
- Advanced option: If a child has memorized a song or short poem, ask the child to recite it, yelling out only the words that rhyme.

Schedule: 10:30 to 11 a.m. At this time, parents and children separate again. In Room A, parents and teachers exchange feedback while the children are enjoying structured playtime in Room B. (See Lesson 1 for more details.)

Lesson 10: Reading with Preschoolers

Materials:
- Standard PCIL materials
- *The Very Hungry Caterpillar* by Eric Carle (video and copies of the book, or a similar title)
- Construction paper
- Scissors
- Glue

Objectives:
Parents will be able to:
- Understand the importance of reading to children.
- Determine how to engage with children when reading a story.

- Remember core questions to ask children about a story.
- Practice with materials to encourage child learning.

Children will be able to:

- Retell the basics of a story.
- Answer basic questions about a story.
- Begin to point out key information from a story.

Schedule: 9 to 9:45 a.m. Again, parents and children gather in separate spaces.

Parents (in Room A)

Tips for Awareness: The teacher goes over tips (like those listed below) as an exercise to encourage conversation and participation within the group, helping to build a safe learning community and introducing parents to these important awareness-raising topics. The teacher should open the discussion by asking parents to contribute their experiences or ideas, and then bring in the relevant information on these topics:

Understanding the importance of reading to young children:

- The development of early literacy skills through early experiences with books and stories is critically linked to a child's success in learning to read.
- Reading aloud to children daily from infancy stimulates early brain development and helps build key language, literacy and social skills.
- Parents should try to read with their children at least once a day at a regularly scheduled time – for example, at bedtime.

Introduction and/or review of Early Learning Content:

- Read *The Very Hungry Caterpillar* by Eric Carle.
- Teach and review words and pronunciation.

Introduction and practice of PCIL activities: The teacher will model an example of reading the book using the strategies to engage children in the story, such as:

- Eliciting some vocabulary from the cover of the book by asking, "What do you see?"
- Reading the story to the children.
- While reading, asking questions about the story, the characters, the setting, what happened and how it ended.
- Having children retell the story one page at a time and predicting what will happen next in the story.
- Having parents explore materials and practice activities. Elicit any other ideas parents may have for using the materials.
- Asking parents to brainstorm how these activities may be used at home, and then give examples.

Discussion, clarifications and questions (see Lesson 1)

Children (in Room B)

Fun introduction to the material: The children's teacher should be introducing the children to the early learning content in a fun and engaging way, including:

- Watching *The Very Hungry Caterpillar* video (or whatever similar book-video you select).
- Using games to practice identifying words and concepts from within the book.

After the fun introduction, the children should sit down together and have a healthy snack before meeting up with their parents.

Schedule: 9:45 to 10:30 a.m. At this time, parents and children come together in one classroom. For the first 20 minutes, we indicate that parents should focus on practicing the Early Learning Content (activities 1-3 below) with their children. For the remaining time, parents should move on to hands-on activities (activities 4-5 below) with their children. Whatever the participants do not get through, we recommend that they try at home.

Parent and Child Interactive Learning activities:

1. Ask questions.
   - Parents elicit some vocabulary from the cover of the book by asking, "What do you see?"
   - As parents read the book, they continue asking, "What do you see?"
   - Parents also ask about the story, characters and setting, with questions such as: "What happened?" "What will happen next?" "How will it end?"
2. Leave out information from the story.
   - Parents read the story to their children again, but this time leave out information and have the children fill in the blanks with their knowledge from the earlier reading.
3. Retell the story.
   - Children are asked to give a description of the story that was read.
   - Children are asked to retell the story page by page.
   - Advanced option: Children are asked about the sequence of the story with questions such as, "What happened first?" "What happened second?"
4. Draw pictures from the story.
   - During a reading of the story, or after the story is finished, children are asked to draw a picture of things that happened in the story.
   - Children are asked to retell the story using the pictures they have drawn.
5. Act out the story.
   - As parents read, children pretend to be the caterpillar and act out each scene of the story.
   - Children are invited to use props from around the room as they act out the story.
   - As an alternative, children are asked to draw, color and cut out materials to illustrate the story.

Schedule: 10:30 to 11 a.m. At this time, parents and children separate again. In Room A, parents and teachers provide feedback to each other while the children are enjoying structured playtime in Room B. (See Lesson 1 for more details.)

Our Partners

Why this matters so much to us

From Dr. Herman B. Gray, President and CEO of United Way for Southeastern Michigan

As the father of two thriving adult children, I fully understand the challenges of parenting. Even under the best of circumstances, parenting is the most difficult, and yet fulfilling, duty that many of us will face.

My wife Shirley and I had it pretty easy with our two girls, but of course, there were always challenges. Homework time was a battleground as the girls struggled with math. These were moments that tested me. (They also proved that I would've made a terribly impatient tutor.) And like many parents, we dealt with stubbornness from our youngest, who pronounced "I know that" to everything that came her way, whether she truly did or not.

I wasn't alone in these moments. As a pediatrician, I saw that the parents of my young patients shared the same worries as me, and I sympathized with them. They would often ask questions like:

"Will they get into the 'right' school?"

"Will they be happy?"

"Will they make a good living?"

My role was to offer non-judgmental support, accurate advice and reassurance. Perhaps one of the greatest parenting challenges is helping our children develop good judgment, moral character and intellectual strength.

It is a tough business raising a child.

Whether a child is 6 or 60, parenting never truly ends, but I am proud to say that both of my girls graduated from the University of Michigan – one earning a master's degree and another a law degree. It makes me proud to see my children passionately pursuing and leading in their careers.

Every child deserves the opportunity to succeed, and it is our collective responsibility to support them. That is why our Social Innovation Fund work is so important. It's structured to create best-in-class practices to help parents and caregivers access the resources and tools needed to support the children in their lives. This work has the potential to not only affect our local community, but it can influence nationwide policy as well.

If we do not move forward to meet the challenges of our ever-changing world, we will fall behind. We cannot be afraid to try new or different approaches to age-old social conditions. Our community's success depends on how we care for and develop our children, which is why it is crucial that we work together and use creative strategies to prepare them for a global future.

My work at United Way for Southeastern Michigan means a great deal to me. I am fully committed to the service of others and to making the world our children live in a better place. We can only carry out this work with our dedicated partners and with the support of our community, and I am grateful for the opportunity we have to collaborate with and learn from one another.

At United Way, we embrace our legacy as leaders in social innovation, and we move forward confidently into an unknown future, growing and learning, and always serving. I hope the books in *The Bib to Backpack Learning Series* will help to guide many parents and community leaders in how we might achieve our goals together – and create a brighter future for our children.

Dr. Herman Gray, MD, MBA is President and CEO of United Way for Southeastern Michigan, appointed to his current post in 2015. Before that, he served as the executive vice president of pediatric health services at the Detroit Medical Center (DMC); prior, he was the DMC Children's Hospital of Michigan's president and chief executive officer for eight years, after serving as its chief operating officer and chief of staff. Dr. Gray's areas of specialty include health care administration, public health, child advocacy and nonprofit management. His medical degree was from the University of Michigan and his Master of Business Administration was from the University of Tennessee. He and his wife, Shirley, have two daughters.

**Tip for Success: Five Themes to Stress With
Your Potential Supporters**

Most nonprofits face the twin challenges of raising
funds and recruiting participants. Consider including
these themes as you reach out:

1. Innovation – How does your team transform and adapt ideas as
   you encounter inevitable challenges?

2. Evidence – How do you know your program works? How
   is your program designed to shift gears on the basis of new
   evidence?

3. Scale – How can your program expand? How do you expect to
   flexibly adapt to the challenges you face as you grow?

4. Match – How can you add additional or matching dollars and
   why will those new funders choose to join your effort?

5. Knowledge Sharing – How are you contributing to the
   widespread sharing of fresh ideas and best practices?

Adapted from the SIF Communicators Toolkit

Tips from United Way and the Social Innovation Fund

In 2009, the Social Innovation Fund (SIF) was launched
through the Corporation for National and Community Service
(CNCS) – the federal agency that sponsors many service programs, including AmeriCorps, Learn and Serve America and
Senior Corps. What made CNCS's new SIF initiative distinctive in the existing array of federal programs was three of its
core goals: a commitment to collaborate with already existing
nonprofits across the country, rather than creating new federal
programs from scratch; a strong mandate to include ongoing
collection of data and evaluation of each funded program to
demonstrate effectiveness; and a pledge to widely share information that could foster scaling and replication of similarly effective

programs. The book you are reading is a major part of United Way for Southeastern Michigan's effort to reach that third goal. The six books in what we are calling *The Bib to Backpack Learning Series* provide transparent and detailed information on how the programs of our six Metro Detroit partners began, how they overcame challenges along the way and how the programs are structured today. The books themselves are easily accessible doorways into the programs – and into the larger potential of the SIF. In addition, by producing high-quality books that share the story of the programs, we also are equipping our six regional nonprofit partners with a valuable tool for their ongoing work with community leaders and funders. Each of these nonprofit groups now can say that they literally are "writing the book" on how to help with early education in challenging neighborhoods through ongoing innovation. That's a major boost in convincing additional partners to support this work.

If you are thinking about developing a program in your region, you also will want to explore the hundreds of pages of tips and detailed analysis of existing programs that are shared by the SIF at http://1.usa.gov/1Sa19iU. These online SIF materials are free to download in PDF format and are packed with helpful information about strategies that already are working in communities from coast to coast. Since one goal of this fund is to encourage robust sharing of information, you may even discover programs in your region that could collaborate with your group in the future.

If you explore the federal website, you will find details on two programs with similar-sounding names that are administered by CNCS. The original 2009 SIF, which is supporting the six programs in southeast Michigan, is sometimes referred to as "SIF Classic" to distinguish it from a new program that was launched in 2014 that is called "SIF Pay for Success." That newer program changes the funding model to leverage federal money only after other organizations have established a program and have proven that it works. The Detroit-area programs are part of the original SIF – but, at this point, either fund may interest community leaders in your part of the country. Both are covered on the federal website.

The following helpful ideas are paraphrased from several public reports, including a late-2015 analysis called *State of the SIF Report*, the *SIF Communicators Toolkit* and a *Lessons and Stories* report, focused on United Way.

Question: Has your involvement with the SIF, including the evaluation component, helped you when meeting with funders?

Answer from UWSEM: Education and youth development is a major focus in our region, and funders also understand the value of SIF. The quality of the SIF's mandated evaluations are especially appealing to many funders who are now expecting to see increased levels of accountability tied to their funds. The national prominence of the SIF, coupled with the fact that this connects with a major focus in our region, has allowed our fund development teams to feel comfortable approaching both funders we work with consistently as well as establishing new relationships with groups that want to contribute to the well-being of children and families in our region.

Question: How has your involvement with the SIF enabled your organization to scale your programs?

Answer from UWSEM: We are continuing to work on scaling efforts with our six programs, including the program that is the subject of this book: ACCESS to School. We work with our six organizations in a collaborative way to set scaling and replication goals and to design action plans to reach those goals. We provide each organization with additional staff hours and technical assistance. In 2016, our major effort toward this goal is the creation of this series of six books that will help community leaders nationwide understand how they could replicate these programs. We are also committed to spreading the use of the valuable Ages and Stages Questionnaire through our BibToBackpack.org website. Plus, we continue to gather new data that help us to identify additional communities in need of these early childhood interventions. That will guide the future placement of resources from our current programs.

Question: When telling the story of an organization's current work and its goals in the future, who should be addressed on a regular basis?

Answer from the SIF: Most organizations maintain a list of "target audiences" as they communicate about their work. Take a look at your list to see if it includes:

- Board members – These leaders set the overall direction of your organization and secure ongoing funding. Members of your board need to understand your work and need to know key details they can share as ambassadors for your program.

- Private funders – Your relationship with your funders doesn't end when the money is provided. These funders are gateways to future funding and they need to know that their money is supporting effective, ongoing work.

- Elected officials – These community leaders can help you overcome barriers and, at some levels of government, may be able to appropriate future funding. Consider scheduling a reception or special program to give elected officials an opportunity to understand your work.

- Program beneficiaries and stakeholders – These men and women embody your impact in the community, but they may not understand the full scope of what you are accomplishing if you don't tell them. Also, help them to understand their ongoing role in telling your group's story.

- Social sector influencers – Are you regularly reaching out to academic institutions, other nonprofit organizations, for-profit social enterprises and other thought leaders in your community? Do you know local journalists and media personalities with an interest in your core community? Many groups overlook valuable contacts with these influential individuals and institutions, partly because you may not be updating and expanding your list of contacts on a regular basis.

Four tips for communicating with your community

1. Communicate regularly – Many organizations are so busy running their programs that they forget there is a larger community that wants to support what they are doing. Consider updates through social media, a monthly newsletter or some other form of ongoing communication.

2. Focus on real people – The strongest public response to your work will come when people see the difference your program makes in the lives of the men, women and children involved. This book is an example of offering human stories as a doorway through which people can explore what you are doing.

3. Share information – Expand the boundaries of your "external communication" to include opportunities for your team to meet with teams from other similar groups. Share innovations and insights.

4. Get creative – Many lengthy reports are generated in a huge program like the SIF. These are essential to track and analyze our evidence, but we also need to find creative, compelling formats for sharing our stories. This series of books is an experiment in sharing of our stories with the world.

Adapted from the SIF Communicators Toolkit

Why United Way is an effective partner

Wherever you are in the world, as you read this book, consider inquiring about the international network of United Way affiliates as a starting point in your efforts to launch a program.

For almost 130 years, United Way affiliates have been leaders in charitable giving focused on meeting pressing community needs in the United States and beyond. Tracing its founding to 1887 in Denver, Colorado, these emerging regional programs bore many names – including Community Chest, a phrase familiar to fans of the classic board game, Monopoly.

A major center in the history of United Way innovation was Detroit, following World War II. That's when financial expert Walter C. Laidlaw adapted lessons from his work with World War II war chest drives to begin building a wide-reaching community consensus that was described in the slogan, "Give Once for All." Laidlaw's reach spanned all levels of the community. For example, he drew avid support from both automotive titan Henry Ford II and pioneering labor leader Walter Reuther. In 1968, Laidlaw retired from his influential role in the organization, and by the 1970s, the phrase "United Way" was becoming widely adopted by the semi-independent affiliates in this worldwide network.

In the late 1980s, criticism arose concerning the way funds were being used in a number of the huge network's American affiliates. At the same time, United Way was facing declines in the automatic donations that had been provided by employees of large corporations since after World War II. As SIF publications describe United Way's history, the organization's 2007 commitment to a new "Community Impact Agenda" was a game-changer in the wake of these problems that had surfaced. One SIF report describes that 2007 change in focus as, "a vision for how United Ways could rebuild trust and remain credible, relevant, and effective." The SIF's analysis continues: "In this vision, United Way affiliates would target a limited number of issues and basic needs whose existence or lack thereof causes or contributes to poverty in communities across the country: income, education, and health. They would look beyond themselves and their network to partner with other grant makers, government agencies, corporations, and nonprofits to concentrate and magnify collective action and investment to tackle difficult social problems."

That's why SIF reports indicate that United Way organizations have proven to be effective partners in this kind of innovative, collaborative program. One SIF report describes the new United Way thinking this way: "United Way would no longer simply write checks to charities and hope they would do what they said they would do; rather, United Way would engage with recipients to strengthen their capacity to implement strong programs. These relationships would move beyond transactional to be transformational." As a result, since 2010, the SIF has funded work through United Way affiliates in parts of Louisiana, Minnesota, Colorado, Ohio, South Carolina, Oregon and Michigan.

However, as anyone who has worked in the nonprofit sector knows, not all grants are immediately accepted. United Way for Southeastern Michigan began its efforts to receive SIF funding in 2010 – but had to retool its application before successfully applying in 2011. If you are considering applying for grants, remember that it takes time, sometimes a period measured in years – and you may need to make repeated attempts, even with a first-rate organization supporting your work.

Overall, the benefits of this partnership have been substantial. A SIF *Lessons and Stories* report describes the impact on the Metro Detroit organization this way:

> The SIF experience had transformative impacts on United Way for Southeastern Michigan (UWSEM) and its sub-grantees. It changed how UWSEM selects grantees, fostered a culture of data-informed decision-making, and bolstered formal and informal knowledge sharing.
>
> "SIF has had both direct and indirect impacts on the way that education work is being done here," said Jennifer Callans, UWSEM's early education director. "The difference between our work before SIF and after is like night and day." …
>
> UWSEM needed to adapt to the SIF's rigorous evaluation requirements by building capacity for itself and for its sub-grantees in key areas such as

data management. UWSEM also needed to align the evaluation activities of its sub-grantees, each of which had its own evaluation plan, third-party evaluator, and data system. To aggregate these different efforts, it worked with its sub-grantees and its portfolio evaluator, Child Trends, to create a common set of outcomes and indicators to serve as the basis for tracking progress across all programs.

If you are reading this book in hopes of launching or expanding a program in your community, many connected with the SIF advise that you first take a close look at the way you collect data about your program and then use it to evaluate your work in an ongoing way. Again, from the Metro Detroit section of the *Lessons and Stories* report:

> The experience with data collection for the SIF grant was informative for everyone, including the sub-grantees, notes Jeffrey Miles, UWSEM's SIF manager.

Tip for Success: Climb Out of Your Silo

Big organizations like United Way can easily fall into silos. We might be funding an agency for something in education, something in basic needs and something in financial stability. Then, we realize all those United Way program officers need to be talking to each other. We've started convening cross-functional teams to share experiences with particular grantees across the organization.

From Jennifer Callans, UWSEM's early education director, in a SIF report.

Tips from our portfolio evaluator

Child Trends, founded in 1979 and based in Bethesda, Maryland, is a leading nonprofit research organization focused on improving public policies and interventions that serve children and families. Programs funded by the SIF are required to conduct rigorous evaluation of their effectiveness, and one part of that effort at UWSEM was to contract with Child Trends, which would conduct ongoing interviews and analysis. The following tips are paraphrased from an interim report by Child Trends, drawing on extensive interviews with professionals working in the various SIF programs in the Detroit area. Although specifically focused on these programs in Southeast Michigan, these tips may be useful to anyone developing such programs in the future.

- **Clear and timely communication is essential.** Good communication is one key to success. Because UWSEM administers various SIF programs, the individual groups developing these programs depend on UWSEM for clear directions and compliance information, as well as updates. Communication also is important in the other direction – so that individual programs can voice their concerns, questions and challenges. One key step UWSEM took was to mandate a series of regular meetings to share updates and to hear what the participants were learning across the spectrum of these local programs.

- **Balance rigor with feasibility when it comes to evaluation plans for the new programs.** All SIF grants require evaluation plans, because the SIF's practice is to support and, ideally, to replicate programs that have clear evidence of success. At the same time, organizers need to understand how these evaluation activities may shape program implementation, which in turn may affect findings in the evaluation. This is a challenging aspect of participating in such a grant, and the six Detroit-area programs all found that they had to pay a great deal of attention to meeting this goal. Organizations trying to develop such programs should not try to go it alone. They should meet as a team, discuss, research and develop strategies that can lead to best practices in evaluating the programs – while, at the same time, not compromising program implementation.

- **Build or improve capacity for data collection and management.** Nonprofits participating in a program like this vary in their capacity to track and manage data. Some have an established data collection infrastructure; others merely collect demographic and/or attendance data. The wide range of capacity in data management poses a challenge to systematically collecting high-quality data across all of the participating programs. To improve data quality, organizations considering such programs should take a close look at their own data management systems and share ideas for improving the management of data with other participating nonprofits. Again, don't go it alone in trying to determine how you will manage your data – share best practices with other organizations to improve everyone's capacity.

- **Tailor expectations of scaling to each program's stage of development.** Everyone hopes that good ideas will flourish and that effective programs will expand – but scaling depends on a program's stage of development. Whether programs ultimately prove effective or not, the fact is that programs don't all develop at the same rate. Some have greater barriers to overcome, while many programs must iron out a long series of glitches. Programs that are relatively new to an organization or community may need to gain experience before they can take off and have a smooth ride. It's critically important to realize that not all programs – even effective ones – will scale at the same rate.

- **Address ongoing funding challenges through collective problem solving.** Detroit is an example of an urban area with limited resources for funding and many nonprofits competing for dollars. UWSEM recognizes that challenge and helps to facilitate funding opportunities. But, even with the best intentions, such efforts sometimes do not prove fruitful. Raising local funds is one of the toughest challenges in this kind of work.

Organizations considering such programs should try to find out how other similar communities are tackling this widespread problem. Sharing advice and opportunities on fundraising leverages collective problem-solving to address this major issue. By collaborating and sharing ideas with other community leaders, you may discover approaches that will help the entire community.

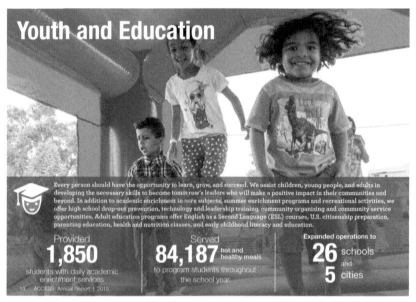

Youth and Education

Every person should have the opportunity to learn, grow, and succeed. We assist children, young people, and adults in developing the necessary skills to become tomorrow's leaders who will make a positive impact in their communities and beyond. In addition to academic enrichment in core subjects, summer enrichment programs and recreational activities, we offer high school drop-out prevention, technology and leadership training, community organizing and community service opportunities. Adult education programs offer English as a Second Language (ESL) courses, U.S. citizenship preparation, parenting education, health and nutrition classes, and early childhood literacy and education.

Provided
1,850
students with daily academic enrichment services

Served
84,187 hot and healthy meals
to program students throughout the school year.

Expanded operations to
26 schools and
5 cities

To learn more about ACCESS, visit www.accesscommunity.org/about/

Acknowledgements

There are countless individuals and partnering organizations whose support of our work has resulted in the writing of this book. First and foremost, we would like to acknowledge that this book would not have been possible without the hard work and dedication of the entire ACCESS Adult and Family Learning team, whose members encourage and inspire our learners every day.

We would like to collectively express our gratitude to the following:

Reading Works, an organization that uses the Collective Impact Model to partner with literacy providers ("Impact Partners"), works toward the common goal of improving adult literacy in Detroit; ACCESS is an Impact Partner with Reading Works, and our ACCESS to School Program has experienced significant impact growth through support from Reading Works.

The PNC Foundation, which has provided funding for the ACCESS to School Program for three years, helping to fund essential program activities, materials, professional development for staff and evaluation.

Detroit Public Schools (DPS), whose partnership during this project has been invaluable. By holding the ACCESS to School Program at Priest Elementary, we have been able to educate parents on the American school system and improve parent engagement at school. We are grateful for the trust and the space to do this work at Priest Elementary. Additionally, we partnered with the Office of Adult Education at DPS to offer English as a Second Language classes to parents on-site at Priest Elementary. Not only does the ACCESS to School Program address school readiness, but with these types of partnerships, it also helps to build trust and relationships between the community and the school systems by empowering parents.

Last, but certainly not least, we would like to recognize the unique opportunity given to us by United Way for Southeastern Michigan (UWSEM) to use our experience and expertise to create the ACCESS to School Program. The opportunity to receive funding from and partner with a regional early childhood champion has been vital to creating this innovative school-readiness initiative. At UWSEM, we especially want to thank Jennifer Callans, Ph.D., Jeffrey D. Miles, MSW, Shaun Taft, LMSW/MSA, Rebecca Tallarigo, BFA/BS, Lindsey Miller, MSW, and Amanda Reed, MPA.

About the Authors

Nahed Alkashbari is a case manager with the ACCESS to School Program. She had a fundamental role in creating the Parent and Child Interactive Learning (PCIL) curriculum, and currently teaches PCIL and parenting education classes. She holds a bachelor's degree in education, and has a long history of working to empower women. Prior to the ACCESS to School Program, Nahed worked with UNICEF, taught as an English as a Second Language (ESL) instructor, educated women and their children on health and nutrition and worked with a micro-finance foundation in Yemen, enabling women to establish and sustain their own businesses.

Amanda Morgan served as supervisor for the Adult and Family Learning programs at ACCESS, which included the ACCESS to School Program. Amanda, together with Nahed, created the PCIL curriculum and program design. She earned her Bachelor of Science in behavioral psychology from Western Michigan University and her Master of Social Work (MSW) from the University of Michigan, where she specialized in program evaluation and community organizing. She is a Licensed Master Social Worker (LMSW) in the State of Michigan and her past work experience includes program management and evaluation, capacity building and organizational development. Amanda currently works at Michigan State University in the

School of Social Work, and continues to serve as a consultant with ACCESS.

Anisa Sahoubah serves as director of the Youth and Education Department at ACCESS and came up with the original idea and funding for the ACCESS to School Program. Anisa earned her bachelor's degree in secondary education and her teaching certification from Wayne State University. She earned a master's degree in adult instruction and performance technology from the University of Michigan. Anisa has helped develop and implement vital programming for the community, building bridges with various community agencies and key stakeholders to maximize the impact of ACCESS programs. Anisa has also led efforts to secure millions of dollars in funding for these programs. In addition to her role as director, Anisa is active in numerous civic, cultural and educational organizations.

Breanne Wainright coordinates the English as a Second Language Program (ESL) at ACCESS. She holds a bachelor's degree in English studies and her certification in Teaching English to Speakers of Other Languages (TESOL). Breanne has taught English in a variety of settings throughout Michigan, successfully teaching students of different cultural backgrounds and language abilities. Breanne became involved with the ACCESS to School Program first as an ESL instructor and facilitator of the children's class in PCIL, then later as the ESL coordinator.

The Bib to Backpack Learning Series

Join us in giving children a great start! Remember: Education begins before school. Research shows that the years between the bib and the backpack make all the difference for school readiness and lifelong success. Let's make those years count!

Making early years matter is our goal at United Way for Southeastern Michigan in launching this new campaign we call

Bib to Backpack. A wide range of informational resources are available for parents and caregivers online at www.BibToBackpack.org. In addition, this Learning Series within the campaign will expand into six individual books throughout 2016, highlighting the inspiring and innovative programs we are sponsoring through the Corporation for National and Community Service's Social Innovation Fund. Sharing these programs with other communities is a major goal of that fund's important work nationwide. We hope that the stories, voices and resources in these books will inspire parents, students, community leaders and professionals nationwide who are looking for fresh ideas to prepare children for school.

CPSIA information can be obtained
at www.ICGtesting.com
Printed in the USA
BVOW11s1002130516

447945BV00004B/5/P